PERSONALITY AND BELIEF

Interdisciplinary Essays on John Henry Newman

EDITED BY

GERARD MAGILL

UNIVERSITY
PRESS OF
AMERICA

Lanham • New York • London

Copyright © 1994 by
University Press of America®, Inc.
4720 Boston Way
Lanham, Maryland 20706

3 Henrietta Street
London WC2E 8LU England

Library of Congress Cataloging-in-Publication Data

Personality and belief : interdisciplinary essays on John Henry
Newman / edited by Gerard Magill.
p.   cm.
Includes bibliographical references.
1. Newman, John Henry, 1801–1890.   2. Theology, Doctrinal—
England—History—19th century.   I. Magill, Gerard.
BX4705.N5P47   1995   282'.092—dc20   94–33440 CIP

ISBN 0–8191–9757–2 (cloth : alk. paper)

Chapter 12, "The Lonergan Connection with Newman's
Grammar" by Carla Mae Streeter was originally published as "The
Newman-Lonergan Connection: Implications for Doing Theology
in North America," in *Current Issues in Catholic Higher
Education* 12:1 (Summer, 1991): 12-16. Reprinted by permission
of the Association of Catholic Colleges and Universities.

 The paper used in this publication meets the minimum requirements of
American National Standard for Information Sciences—Permanence
of Paper for Printed Library Materials, ANSI Z39.48–1984.

To Aunt Mae and Catherine

CONTENTS

Abbreviations of Newman's Works

The standard abbreviations of the works of John Henry Newman are adopted in this collection.

Apo.   *Apologia Pro Vita Sua: Being a History of His Religious Opinions*

Ari.   *The Arians of the Fourth Century*

AW   *John Henry Newman: Autobiographical Writings*, ed. Henry Tristram

Call.   *Callista, A Sketch of the Third Century*
                In the later editions of 1889, 1890:
                Callista, a Tale of the Third Century

Campaign   *My Campaign in Ireland, Part I*

Cons.   *On Consulting the Faithful in Matters of Doctrine*, ed. John Coulson

DA   *Discussions and Arguments on Various Subjects*

Dev.   *An Essay on the Development of Christian Doctrine*

Diff. I, II   *Certain Difficulties Felt by Anglicans in Catholic Teaching.* 2 vols.

Ess. I, II   *Essays Critical and Historical.* 2 vols.

Acknowledgments

I am most grateful to Saint Louis University for enabling me to organize the Newman Centenary Conference in Fall 1990, from which I have selected the essays in this collection. All of these essays were written originally for the conference. I thank my graduate assistants Peter Huff, Joffrey Hermsen and Marianne Sheahan for their attentive reading of the entire manuscript and astute observations about textual changes for the graduate reader. Also, I am grateful to the Mellon Faculty Development Committee at Saint Louis University for awarding me a grant to prepare this volume. A collection of different essays from this conference also has been published: Gerard Magill, *Discourse and Context: An Interdisciplinary Study of John Henry Newman* (Carbondale, IL: Southern Illinois University Press, 1993).

The following essay in this collection has appeared elsewhere. Carla Mae Streeter's "The Lonergan Connection with Newman's *Grammar*," was published as "The Newman-Lonergan Connection," in *Current Issues in Catholic Higher Education*, 12, no. 1 (Summer, 1991): 12–16.

Introduction: Newman's Sense
of Personal Belief

Gerard Magill

A sense of personal belief inspired John Henry Newman (1801–90), especially in his lifelong commitment to explaining the interaction between reason and religion. This sense was the driving force of his conversion from Anglicanism to Catholicism in 1845, the leitmotif of his religious epistemology in the *Grammar of Assent* (1870)[1] which was the philosophical fruition of his earlier Oxford *University Sermons* (1826–43),[2] and a recurrent theme throughout his very personal *Letters and Diaries*,[3] all of which are examined in this collection.

Unfortunately, as a young scholar at Oxford he fell under the alluring sway of rationalism in the form of religious liberalism: "I was drifting in the direction of the Liberalism of the day" (*Apo.*, 26).[4] At Oriel College, where he was appointed Fellow in 1822, he had been attracted excessively to the persuasive logic of Richard Whately (1787–1863). However, as early as 1826, in a university sermon, preached before he became Vicar of St. Mary's, Newman openly resisted what he called the "unhesitating reliance on our own acuteness and powers of reasoning" in religious faith (*Sermons*, 8). Instead, he alluded to another mode of reasoning, appealing "to the strength of . . . accumulated probabilities" (*Sermons*, 15), which he later defined as "informal inference" in distinction from the formal inference of logic (*Grammar*, 288). This "living personal reasoning" (*Grammar*, 300), described by Edward Sillem as Newman's "personal liberalism,"[5] became the mainstay of his sense of personal belief.

Newman preferred concrete and personal reasoning (personal liberalism) to abstract and deductive logic (the rationalism of liberalism) in religion. He understood that both modes of reasoning were necessary for true perception, but he gave priority to the former as "the real method of reasoning" (*Grammar*, 292) to justify belief. There was a reciprocity, then, between his sense of personal belief and his method of personal reasoning, each illumining the other throughout his writings.

These essays examine from an interdisciplinary perspective Newman's sense of personal belief. The book's title, *Personality and Belief*, has both descriptive and prescriptive purposes. Descriptively, the title suggests the influence of Newman's personality upon his preferred mode of reasoning to justify his personal belief. Prescriptively, and more importantly, the title refers to the normative relation between personality and belief in the sense of adopting personal reasoning to warrant religious faith.

This collection arises from papers presented during the Newman Centenary Conference at Saint Louis University in Fall 1990. In this introductory essay I consider the three organizing divisions of the collection to elucidate the rapport between personality and belief in Newman's thought. First, his own personality sets the background for appreciating his sense of belief. Second, his personal principle of reasoning shapes both his philosophy and theology. Third, his justification of personal belief was an original argument whose fundamental insight remains relevant today. The epilogue celebrates the centenary year of Newman's death.

I

Newman's sense of personal belief was a subtle achievement that reflected his complex personality. The essays in the first division of this collection consider his personality and achievement. To begin from a generic standpoint, Ian Ker ("The Greatness of Newman") examines Newman's interdisciplinary accomplishment. As a philosopher, Newman's insight into the nature of the human mind, especially in the *Grammar*, challenged the epistemology of the Enlightenment: he used personal reasoning to create hypotheses (based on assumptions) that accounted for data through an accumulation of probabilities, thereby anticipating crucial elements in twentieth century philosophy of science. As a theologian he applied his philosophy of mind especially to doctrine in *An Essay on the Development of Doctrine* (1845)[6] and to ecclesiology in the 1877 Preface to the *Via Media*.[7] In that Preface he presented a creative dialectic between church authority and individual intellect, a tension that remains a major source of controversy in theology over a century later. As an educator he applied his theory of knowledge to liberal education in the Dublin University discourses (1852), later published as the first part of the *Idea of a University* (1873).[8] In that work, by cultivating the intellect through training the mind to think clearly, to evaluate, and to judge, he anticipated basic questions in the philosophy of education today. Moreover, he applied his preoccupation with the mind as a pastor, providing sound pastoral and psychological insight in his *Parochial and Plain Sermons*,[9] and as a writer, rhetorically mastering intellectual satire in his *Lectures on the Present Position of Catholics*.[10]

Newman's growth to greatness accords with a personality whose psychological profile is addressed by Ronald R. Burke ("Newman: The Man Behind the Cloud"). In light of personality theory, Newman's ambiguous relations with his family, including many stories of enduring difficulties, diverse features of his personal profile as a reformer can be identified. He was principled and orderly with a powerful commitment to morality and conscience, being both compulsive and hardworking. He was also stubborn and strong willed, nurturing a stoic perfectionism that was characterized as much by denouncing the world (with an inspiring selflessness) as by repressing his emotions (under a noble, philosophical demeanor). Alongside these features of his personality, Joseph H. Wessling ("The Androgynous Ideal: Newman's *Callista*") explores Newman's masculine and feminine psychological traits in his novel. The novel *Callista*, set near Carthage at the onset of the Decian persecution in the early Church, was started in 1848 but was not completed until 1855.[11]   Though Newman never addressed androgyny formally, in the Dublin discourses of the *Idea* the androgynous personality was indispensable both for the wholeness of the gentleman (being decisive yet gentle) and of society.   In the following year his novel *Callista* moved beyond the *Idea* by developing the androgynous ideal in women (Callista), associating this ideal with the Christian faith. Despite this intentional shift in sensitivity to women in his novel, he never engaged actively with the advancement of women. Yet Joyce Sugg ("Newman and the Intellectual Advancement of Women") suggests that Newman's respect for women was obvious not only in entrusting the compilation of his selected letters to Anne Mozley but also in his close friendships with, for example, Emily Bowles and Charlotte Wood, with whom he shared many of his personal crises.

Newman's personality was prone to crises which were catalysts for much of his achievement.   Eugene Hollahan ("Newman's Crisis-Trope in the *Apologia*") argues that the crisis-trope appears to structure his autobiography.   Like many nineteenth century authors Newman was thrown into crisis by dominant ideologies, in his case religious liberalism, and he used the crisis-trope to make the transition from Protestantism to Catholicism.   In particular, George Eliot's use of crisis as a master trope in 1866, signifying both anxiety and response, illumines the crisis-trope in Newman's *Apologia* as a method both for making statements and dealing with reality. It was by bringing his own personality to bear upon his fundamental mode of arguing that Newman confidently proposed a personal principle of reasoning that pervaded his philosophy and theology in general and inspired his sense of belief in particular.

II

Newman's personal principle weaves together the essays in the second division of this collection: the close rapport between his personalism and liberalism illumines his approach to catechesis and his response to religious prejudice.   Marie Brinkman ("Newman's Personal Principle at its Source") offers an explanation of Newman's experience, especially regarding the type of reasoning that rooted his intellectual and religious growth. His personal principle referred to the personal influence that shaped his sense of personal belief. This principle elaborated upon his view of liberal knowledge and judgment in the *Idea* to elicit the informal reasoning of the illative sense in the *Grammar*. Harvey Kerpneck ("Newman and Arnold: Liberalism Tempered by Reflection") shows that Newman's personal principle in religion had a formative influence upon Matthew Arnold.   For both men the link between liberal education and religious judgment inspired a sense of personal belief that motivated a liberal, humanistic stance.   Newman's catechesis was rooted in this principle of reasoning and belief.   Günter Biemer ("Newman's Catechesis in a Pluralistic Age") discusses the significance of this personal principle for Newman's catechesis, arguing that it was a model of interpersonal learning that characterized the theory of education in the Dublin discourses. Newman recognized this method of catechesis for the laity as appropriate for teaching Christianity in a pluralistic age and also as helpful for responding to one-sided criticism of religion. Also, Jay Newman ("Newman's Advice to Victims of Anti-Catholic Prejudice") investigates Newman's personal principle of belief as the intellectual foundation of his view of religious prejudice. Because John Henry Newman's view of prejudice was epistemological at root, he responded by turning to his personal principle of reasoning: personal influence through direct contact would educate prejudiced minds and therefore illumine antagonistic, religious belief.

III

The third division of essays in this collection deals with Newman's justification of personal belief. The explanation of liberal education in the Dublin discourses of the *Idea* was crucial for the elaboration of personal reasoning and religious judgment in the *Grammar*. Michael Martin ("Enlargement of Mind and Religious Judgment in *Loss and Gain*" [1848][12]) studies this connection. In this novel Newman presented religious judgment in a remarkably similar way to his later account in the Dublin University discourses where he defined liberal education as the enlargement of mind, a philosophical habit of mind. This mental enlargement prescribed the growth of knowledge (liberal education) as being capable of reasoning well and of perceptive judgment. In *Loss and Gain* religious development progresses just like knowledge in the *Idea*: opinions in religion are ordered by a creed just as knowledge is ordered by the philosophical habit of mind in the university. Hence, in his novel, Catholicism is not merely a list of doctrinal principles, just as in his discourses philosophical knowledge is not merely a set of logical conclusions. Both religious judgment and the enlargement of mind require the personal principle of reasoning.

Similarly, Edward Enright ("The Letters to Charles Newman as Background to the *Grammar*") indicates that Newman's sense of belief was rooted in personal reasoning. In the *Grammar* Newman argued that informal inference justified religious assent. His intermittent letters between 1823–30 to his brother, Charles Robert, who rejected Christianity, provide a valuable source for his later understanding of the reasonableness of belief. In this correspondence John Henry Newman explained that to justify faith the intellect's reasoning and judgment must be guided by a moral disposition. Later, in the *Grammar*, this disposition enables personal reasoning (informal inference) to discern when the available evidence for revelation, even though not logically compelling, is sufficient to attain religious truth (assent).

This justification of personal belief in the *Grammar* was a creative and original argument. Carla Mae Streeter ("The Lonergan Connection with Newman's *Grammar*") demonstrates its relevance today both for epistemology and theology. Newman and the Canadian philosopher Bernard Lonergan adopted a similar method in cognitional theory. They opposed relativism, charted the concrete operation of the mind seeking truth, and began from experience to reach certainty by developing a religious epistemology based upon the empirical data of consciousness. In particular, the role of Newman's illative sense in the dynamism of faith (personal reasoning warranting religious assent) significantly influenced Lonergan's reflective act of understanding and explanation of insight. Further, as Newman's argument was based upon the accumulation of probabilities, Lonergan also argued from cumulative and progressive results. Their empirical method has significant implications for theology today by promoting a dialogue between theology and the natural sciences and by establishing a coherent role for reason in religious belief.

In sum, the reciprocity between Newman's sense of personal belief and his personal principle of reasoning inspired a method for justifying religious faith that enthralled his readers over a century ago and is captivating for scholars today. That accomplishment is celebrated by Sheridan Gilley ("Newman: A Toast") in the collection's epilogue. *Personality and Belief*, then, is a title portraying the personal dynamism of Newman's thought that is the inspiration of these interdisciplinary essays honoring the centenary year of his death.

Notes

1. John Henry Newman, *An Essay in Aid of a Grammar of Assent*, edited, introduction, and notes by I. T. Ker (Oxford: Clarendon Press, 1985).

2. *Newman's University Sermons. Fifteen Sermons Preached before the University of Oxford, 1826–43*, with introductory essays by D. M. MacKinnon and J. D. Holmes (London: S.P.C.K., 1970).

3. *The Letters and Diaries of John Henry Newman*, ed. C. S. Dessain et al., 31 vols. Vols. I–VI (Oxford: Clarendon Press, 1978–84); Vols. XI–XXII (London: Oxford University Press, 1961–72); Vols. XXIII–XXXI (Oxford: Clarendon Press,

1973–77).

4. John Henry Newman, *Apologia Pro Vita Sua*, edited, introduction, and notes by Martin J. Svaglic (Oxford: Clarendon Press, 1967). See, Gerard Magill, "Imaginative Moral Discernment: Newman on the Tension Between Reason and Religion," *The Heythrop Journal* XXXII (1991): 493–510.

5. *The Philosophical Notebook of John Henry Newman*, 2 vols., ed. Edward J. Sillem (Louvain: Nauwelaerts Publishing House, 1969), I, 67–148, especially 86, 119. See, Gerard Magill, "Newman's Personal Reasoning: The Inspiration of the Early Church," *Irish Theological Quarterly* 58/4 (1992) 305–13.

6. John Henry Newman, *An Essay on the Development of Doctrine* (Notre Dame, IN: University of Notre Dame Press, 1989). See, Gerard Magill, "Interpreting Moral Doctrine: Newman on Conscience and Law," *Horizons* 20/1 (1993): 7–22.

7. John Henry Newman, *The VIA MEDIA of the Anglican Church*, edited, introduction, and notes by H. D. Weidner (Oxford: Clarendon Press, 1990). See, Gerard Magill, "Moral Imagination in Theological Method and Church Tradition: John Henry Newman," *Theological Studies* 53 (1992): 451–75.

8. John Henry Newman, *The Idea of a University*, edited, introduction, and notes by I. T. Ker (Oxford: Clarendon Press, 1976). See, Gerard Magill, "Newman on Liberal Education and Moral Pluralism," *Scottish Journal of Theology* 45 (1992): 45–64.

9. John Henry Newman, *Parochial and Plain Sermons*, 8 volumes from 1834 (London: Longmans, Green, 1891).

10. John Henry Newman, *Lectures on the Present Position of Catholics in England*, addressed to the Brothers of the Oratory, 1851 (London: Longmans, Green, 1899).

11. John Henry Newman, *Callista: A Tale of the Third Century* (London: Burns and Oates, no date).

12. John Henry Newman, *Loss and Gain* (London: James Burns, 1848; reprinted New York: Garland Press, 1975).

Part I

Personality

1

The Greatness of Newman
Ian Ker

During this centenary year much interest has been expressed in the significance of Newman for both the Anglican Communion and the Catholic Church. As the leader and master mind of the Oxford or Tractarian Movement, Newman helped to transform the Church of England, while his resistance to Ultramontanism led him to espouse theological positions which finally received formal approval at the Second Vatican Council of which Newman has often been called the father. My purpose, however, is not to speak of either the Anglican or the Catholic Newman, except incidentally. Rather, I wish to examine the greatness of Newman as a universal figure whose achievement far surpasses the particular religious preoccupations of the time in which he lived.

There are five main, if not equally important, areas where Newman's achievement was outstanding and produced works which are established intellectual and literary classics. I propose, accordingly, to consider Newman as a philosopher, as a theologian, as an educator, as a preacher, and as a writer, in that order.

I. Newman as Philosopher

I start with Newman's philosophy because so much of his most distinctive intellectual contribution rests on his understanding of the nature of the human mind, a conception which he first set forth in the *Oxford University Sermons*,[1] a book which is the most seminal of his works, where we find the key ideas which were to inform not only his later philosophical thought in *An Essay in Aid of a Grammar of Assent*, but also his theology and educational writings.

The view of the human mind that Newman adumbrated with such brilliance and originality in these sermons was a direct challenge to the narrow epistemology that had dominated Western thinking since the Enlightenment, in which rationality was limited to strictly deductive or inductive thinking. As a young man in his early twenties, Newman was confronted in a personal way with religious unbelief by his younger brother Charles, who had become skeptical about Christianity. His letters to his brother at that time mark the beginning of a lifetime of apologetic writing which eventually culminated in the *Grammar of Assent*. What is particularly interesting about this youthful correspondence is the way in which Newman probes beneath the surface of the outward arguments for and against religious belief to discover the real reasons which actually influence people in their thinking. The remarkably penetrating observations in these letters foreshadow the profound insights of the *Oxford University Sermons*. What is it that really determines whether a person is or is not a religious believer? Not, says Newman, the explicit and ostensible arguments advanced, but rather a person's fundamental assumptions and expectations which are normally not directly adverted to at all. The realization that such intellectual differences between people in fact rest on states of mind not open to obvious view came early to Newman. He saw very clearly that without what he called "first principles" it would be impossible to think at all. Such an epistemological approach certainly did not tally very well with the simplistic confidence of nineteenth-century science in the possibility of the straightforward attainment of truth, but it does seem to accord rather closely with the view of later twentieth-century philosophers of science that scientific knowledge develops on the basis of hypotheses which, having been tested rather than strictly proven, appear best to account for the observable phenomena, but which never have been actually demonstrated to be true.

Newman thought that religious belief is no different from other beliefs in being formed less by actual arguments than by what he called "antecedent probabilities," that is, by what we think likely to be true on the basis of our already existing assumptions and attitudes. It is these that not only determine our evaluation of the arguments for and against, but also make us decide that the formal arguments are compelling even though they fall short of positive proof. The arguments themselves, however, are not of no consequence and may exist, albeit implicitly, even in someone who has never explicitly entertained them.

Refusing to accept the limited post-Enlightenment concept of reason and rationality, Newman's achievement in the *Oxford University Sermons* is to redefine the rational in the larger sense of the reasonable. His immediate purpose, of course, is to show that religious belief (and unbelief is no different), far from being the only kind of reasoning which Cartesian rationalism or Lockean empiricism would consider irrational, is in fact only like our other most important beliefs which we do not doubt to be true and yet which we cannot prove, either deductively or inductively, to be true. One obvious reaction to the emphasis the eighteenth-century, the "age of reason," had placed on the evidences for Christianity, was to stress a religion of feelings. Newman's response, however, was not to take the romantic road of Schleiermacher, but instead his originality lay in conceiving of reasoning in a more generous way than had been current since the seventeenth-century. The following passage may be evocative in an almost poetic way, but as a phenomenological description of the workings of the intellect its realism does justice to the complexity of the intellect in a way that a philosopher like Locke never attempted:

> The mind ranges to and fro, and spreads out, and advances forward with a quickness which has become a proverb, and a subtlety and versatility which baffle investigation. It passes on from point to point, gaining one by some indication; another on a probability; then availing itself of an association; then

falling back on some received law; next seizing on testimony; then committing itself to some popular impression, or some inward instinct, or some obscure memory; and thus it makes progress not unlike a climber on a steep cliff, who, by quick eye, prompt hand, and firm foot, ascends how he knows not himself, by personal endowments and by practice, rather than by rule, leaving no track behind him, and unable to teach another. It is not too much to say that the stepping by which great geniuses scale the mountains of truth is as unsafe and precarious to men in general, as the ascent of a skillful mountaineer up a literal crag. It is a way which they alone can take; and its justification lies in their success. And such mainly is the way in which all men, gifted or not gifted, commonly reason, - not by rule, but by an inward faculty. (*US*, 257)

Newman's phenomenology is, then, a much richer thing than the epistemology of the Enlightenment. The implicit reference to the imagination in the above passage looks forward to the later famous distinction between the categories of real and notional apprehension and assent. Another crucial element in Newman's strategy in redefining and enlarging—or rather restoring—our concept of human intelligence can be seen in his stress on the mind as active rather than passive, dynamic rather than static. It is not just that the mind evaluates, imagines, and intuits, as well as deducing and inferring, but it takes the initiative and bears a personal responsibility in attaining to the kind of truths that are not encompassed by logic or sense-perception. According to the personalist philosophy that Newman develops in the *Grammar of Assent*, the mind (or what he calls the "illative sense") reaches certainty in all the important questions of life, including religion, by personally weighing up the various factors and judging whether the balance of probabilities is sufficiently overwhelming in favor of a particular truth.

Newman's philosophy of religion found no more favor with Catholic scholasticism than it did with Anglo-Saxon empiricism. But thanks to modern philosophical movements, such as existentialism, personalism, and phenomenology, his ideas have assumed a new interest, while his common-sense critique of skepticism, for example, bears a striking resemblance to the approach of the later Wittgenstein. However, my concern now is not to develop these points of comparison but to show how central Newman's fascination with the mind is to his non-philosophical work.

II. Newman as Theologian

The last of the *Oxford University Sermons* is a lengthy discussion of the problem of doctrinal development. Not only is it one of the most brilliant of Newman's writings, but it contains within it the essential ideas of *An Essay on the Development of Christian Doctrine*, his most celebrated theological work and a kind of counterpart to Darwin's *Origin of Species*. The sermon exemplifies the philosophy of mind developed in the earlier sermons and provides the key to understanding the *Essay* itself, which, far from being a work of abstract, systematic theology, suggests by virtue of its very literary texture that the right approach to this crucial theological subject is not to attempt a theoretical solution but to examine the historical phenomena, not in a clinically analytical way but by applying the imagination in such a way as to make the history of doctrinal development come alive. Furthermore, if the Christian Church can be said to have a mind, then its mind will be like the individual mind of the believer already depicted in the earlier sermons on faith and reason. In particular, for example, its knowledge is not only explicit but also implicit. Thus, the fact that the early Church was not conscious of later defined dogmas does not necessarily mean that it was not cognizant of them. Rather, what was implicitly believed becomes explicitly professed, as Newman makes clear in the following passage which he quotes in the *Essay* from the sermon and which he introduces by commenting that in theology the mind develops "the solemn ideas, which it has hitherto held implicitly and without subjecting them to its reflecting and reasoning powers."

The mind which is habituated to the thought of God, of Christ, of the Holy Spirit, naturally turns with a devout curiosity to the contemplation of the object of its adoration, and begins to form statements concerning it, before it knows whither, or how far, it will be carried. One proposition necessarily leads to another, and a second to a third; then some limitation is required; and the combination of these opposites occasions some fresh evolutions from the original idea, which indeed can never be said to be entirely exhausted. This process is its development, and results in a series, or rather body of dogmatic statements, till what was an impression on the Imagination has become a system or creed in the reason.

As God is one, so the impression which He gives us of Himself is one. . . . It is the vision of an object. . . . Creeds and dogmas live in the one idea which they are designed to express, and which alone is substantive. (*Dev.*, 52–53)

These last sentences reveal a personalist (as opposed to propositional) theology of revelation which hardly accords with the neo-scholasticism of the Church Newman was soon to join but which, like his philosophy of personalism, strikes a very modern chord in a revived Catholic theology drawing its inspiration, like Newman's own theology, from the scriptural and patristic sources.

Theologians who have looked to the *Essay* to provide a *theory* of development have not only failed to take account of the significance of the word *essay* in the title but have missed Newman's point which is that history shows that those doctrinal developments that have taken place are not susceptible of a systematic analysis for the simple reason that what is unsystematic of its nature does not yield to systematic treatment.

The development . . . of an idea is not like an investigation worked out on paper, in which each successive advance is a pure evolution from a foregoing, but it is carried on through and by means of communities of men and their leaders and guides; and it employs their minds as its instruments, and depends upon them, while it uses them. (*Dev.*, 38)

Christianity, then, is not an abstract concept, the developments of which may be logically deduced in scholastic fashion from the original deposit of faith, but is a living idea depending for its life on a living community, the Church. Newman once remarked that he thought that as an Anglican theologian he had been the first writer to make *life* one of the notes of the Church. Certainly, as a Catholic theologian his ecclesiology is original and valuable precisely because he refuses to regard the Church as a lifeless institution for which theological blue-prints are possible, let alone suitable. The reason why there are theoretically insoluble problems in the Church is because it has an extremely complex life like all living organisms. As a Tractarian or Anglo-Catholic Newman had been preoccupied with the fear that the so-called "Via Media" of the Oxford movement, between Rome on the one hand and Protestantism on the other, was *unreal* because it was a mere academic theory which had never really been put into practice, and if it was would not work. This preoccupation with the real, with the actual and the practical, he was to retain in his Catholic thinking on the nature of the Church.

The last great chapter of the *Apologia Pro Vita Sua*, where Newman turns to a general defense of the Roman Catholic Church, having concluded the account of his own personal religious history, contains some of the most marvelous prose he ever wrote. The power of the rhetoric depends on a sharply antithetical dialectic, as Newman contrives to hold a carefully poised balance between conservative and liberal Catholicism. But it is not a fudged compromise or a woolly comprehensiveness that is aimed at. For Newman refuses to accept that there are only two alternatives, with the further possibility of a middle way between the two extreme positions. This might be the case if the human mind worked in the limited, mechanical grooves of the Enlightenment. But if so much depends on the particular orientation of the individual mind in the personal attainment of truth, so too general intellectual horizons change as perspectives alter. And just as Newman liked to picture the progress of the intellect in terms of struggle, so too it is so often for him the direct conflict between diametrically opposed points of view that causes the crucial shift of the perspective that then allows the apparently intractable problem to be seen in a new light and so to be resolved, in a way that would be impossible for an epistemology that does not allow the mind to see.

In his defense of the Catholic belief in the Church's infallibility, Newman calls it a "power . . . happily adapted to be a working instrument . . . for smiting hard and throwing back the immense energy of the aggressive, capricious, untrustworthy intellect." But in spite of the severely uncompromising defense of the Church's authority, both infallible and non-infallible, that follows, Newman is completely candid about the inevitable objection that "the restless intellect of our common humanity is utterly weighed down" by such an imperious authority, "so that, if this is to be the mode of bringing it into order, it is brought into order only to be destroyed." Against this criticism Newman sets the claim that in fact the "energy of the human intellect . . . thrives and is joyous, with a tough elastic strength, under the terrible blows of the divinely-fashioned weapon, and is never so much itself as when it has lately been overthrown." The resolution of this apparent contradiction lies in the remarkable argument that far from being mutually contradictory, church authority and individual reason need each other precisely because paradoxically, each is actually sustained by conflict with the other.

> It is the vast Catholic body itself, and it only, which affords an avenue for both combatants in that awful, never-dying duel. It is necessary for the very life of religion . . . that the warfare should be incessantly carried on. Every exercise of Infallibility is brought out into act by an intense and varied operation of the Reason, both as its ally and as its opponent, and provokes again, when it has done its work, a re-action of Reason against it; and as in a civil polity the State exists and endures by means of the rivalry and collision, the

encroachments and defeats of its constituent parts, so in like manner Catholic Christendom is no simple exhibition of religious absolutism, but presents a continuous picture of Authority and Private Judgement alternately advancing and retreating as the ebb and flow of the tide; - it is a vast assemblage of human beings with wilful intellects and wild passions, brought together into one by the beauty and the Majesty of a Superhuman Power, - into what may be called a large reformatory or training-school, not as if into a hospital or into a prison, not in order to be sent to bed, not to be buried alive, but (if I may change my metaphor) brought together as if into some moral factory, for the melting, refining, and moulding by an incessant, noisy process, of the raw material of human nature, so excellent, so dangerous, so capable of divine purposes. (*Apo.*, 225-26)[2]

Again, what emerges from these last pages of the *Apologia* is not anything in the nature of a systematic theology of the teaching authority of the Catholic Church. But then, the whole implication of the rhetoric of the argument is that there is an important sense in which it is inappropriate to seek any kind of blue-print for the relation between authority and freedom in the Church. The point of Newman's carefully balanced dialectic is that it is impossible either to describe or to prescribe exactly how this aspect of the Church's life is lived or ought to be lived.

As in Newman's philosophy, so in his theology is to be found an important appeal to common sense. After the controversial definition of papal infallibility at the First Vatican Council, Newman was quick to point out the actual limitations in practice of the doctrine. Like laws, the teachings of popes and councils require interpretation; they cannot interpret themselves. Indeed, these teachings require in the first place the recognition of the Church that they are actually what they purport to be, authentic teachings; they are obviously not in themselves self-legitimizing. This common-sense theology of "reception" does not mean that a pope has to get permission from the rest of the Church before making a dogmatic definition; but it does mean that he can hardly define as a point of faith something which the

Church does not in fact believe. Again, when it is a question of authoritative moral teaching, it is hardly more than a matter of common sense that the individual conscience is still required to apply the general principle to the concrete case and the actual agent: does this particular false statement count as a lie, and if it does can it be justified as a means of preventing a greater evil? In these most controverted aspects of Catholic life Newman's shrewd practical observations still have great relevance.

Newman's last important theological work, the lengthy 1877 preface to a new edition of his Anglican *Lectures on the Prophetical Office*, completes his Catholic theology of the Church. Its ostensible purpose is to explain corruptions in Catholicism; its achievement is to offer in the place of the usual schematic, juridical ecclesiology a less systematic, more subtle view of the actual workings of the Church which exhibits the same kind of inconsistencies to which any living organism is liable. Like Christ who is at one and the same time prophet, priest, and king, so the Church has to exercise simultaneously the three disparate offices of teaching, ruling and worshipping. The three quite distinct offices are based on different principles and are subject to different corruptions. Thus theology tends to rationalism, devotion to superstition, and power to ambition. The extreme difficulty of combining all three offices is well illustrated by Newman's practical question, "What line of conduct, except on the long, the very long run, is at once edifying, expedient, and true?" Eschewing theory in favor of concrete examples, including some telling ones drawn from the New Testament, Newman shows how the three offices are both separate and yet interconnected. The essay's conclusion that "whatever is great refuses to be reduced to human rule" again stresses the limitations of the kind of scholastic theology that would provide the sort of blue-print that is in fact an inappropriate form of description of the complex life of the Church, of which the tension between the three offices is a creative and integral part.[3]

III. Newman as Educator

It is time to return to Newman's philosophy of the mind and to the *Oxford University Sermons*, where the description of the so-called philosophical mind in the penultimate sermon on "Wisdom, as contrasted with Faith and with Bigotry," anticipates the essence of Newman's idea of a university. Like nearly all Newman's works, *The Idea of a University* is an occasional work: the first half consists of the *Discourses on the Scope and Nature of University Education*, the lectures that Newman was commissioned to deliver as a prelude to launching the new Catholic University of Ireland. The second half, which is much less well-known (indeed, in talking about the *Idea of a University*, people often mean simply the *Discourses*), consists of a fairly miscellaneous collection of talks and articles which Newman wrote as the founding President of the University. In fact, the *Lectures and Essays*, as they are called, are generally more practical and usefully complement the more theoretical *Discourses*. The fact is that the *Idea of a University*, although it may be the one recognized classic on the subject, is very far from being a systematic treatise on education.

It is true that according to Newman the purpose of university education is to cultivate what he calls (with an element of hyperbole) the "philosophy of an imperial intellect," but this philosophy turns out to be not some kind of super-philosophy or master-science but rather more simply that "real cultivation of mind" which he explains is "the intellect . . . properly trained and formed to have a connected view or grasp of things" (*Idea*, 10-11).[4] The popular conception of Newman's purpose in the *Idea of a University* is that he wanted to advocate the study of the traditional arts subjects, that is the classics, as the central aim of a university education. Those, on the other hand, who have actually studied the *Discourses* have often concluded that Newman's real intention is to install theology as the queen of the sciences. Needless to say, there is some truth in both of these misconceptions. Newman's original brief was certainly to defend the value of a Catholic university and to justify the teaching of theology as an academic subject. This brief he executed with great eloquence undoubtedly; but although he argued vehemently that theology is a genuine branch of knowledge and should therefore be studied as a subject of study at university and although of course he regarded the subject matter of theology as uniquely important—still he did not advocate the study of theology as central to a liberal education. On the other hand, although he saw no reason why the traditional liberal arts should not continue to be valued as the best instruments of education, he was also quite open to the possibility that other subjects might achieve the same result.

What, then, for Newman was the end of a university education? The simple answer is: to train the mind. But, as we have seen, Newman's idea of the mind was much richer than what often passes for the mind. And this is the answer to those who see the *Idea of a University* as essentially a reactionary celebration of the old Oxford Greats-trained mind, that is a mind that has been taught by means of the classics to express itself precisely, to think logically, and to argue clearly from well-marshalled evidence. True, such lucidity and precision are indeed absolutely central to Newman's idea. This interpretation, then, is much closer to Newman's meaning than the popular notion that the *Idea of a University* is concerned to advocate the kind of culture which results from studying subjects like history and literature. Actually it is noticeable that in spite of several discussions of the educational value of studying literature, there is no attempt to claim that literary studies have a *cultural* value, in the sense in which we use that word today. For Newman it is not an education in the liberal arts as such which constitutes a liberal education, but rather it is the intellectual formation traditionally connected with the study of the liberal arts that makes a liberal education. This is why theology, although far more important as a branch of knowledge, is for Newman inferior educationally speaking to the study of the classical languages, literature, and thought. If it could be shown that a scientific or theological course of studies can train the mind as effectively, then it would be considered by Newman to provide a no less so-called liberal education. Whatever the value inherent in the subject matter of arts subjects—and of course Newman would be the last person to despise such a value—that is not his chief concern: it is not culture that he is concerned with, but the training of the mind. And it is important to emphasize that this training of the mind does not mean studying logic, let alone studying how to think, for one learns to think not by learning a science of thinking but by actually thinking about specific subjects of knowledge.

However, if clear thinking is of the essence of a well-trained mind, it does not by itself constitute the properly educated mind, any more than the mind itself is confined only to strictly deductive and inductive thinking. Because the intellect is dynamic rather that static, education must stress "the power of initiation" (*Idea*, 126), for one can only become educated by actively using one's own mind oneself as opposed to passively absorbing information. Again, what Newman calls "the cultivation of the intellect" includes the ability not only to "grasp things as they are" but also "of arranging things according to their real value." It is not only a matter of "clearsightedness," since the "sagacity" or "wisdom" which is supposed to be conferred by education involves too "an acquired faculty of judgement." For the educated person is required not only to think clearly but also to evaluate and to judge. Thus, while logical lucidity is an essential attribute of the educated mind, so too is the power of distinguishing priorities, of seeing what is important and significant and what is not, of making the kind of evaluations that will certainly greatly vary from subject to subject but which are inseparable from the decision-making which is inherent in all acquisitions of advances in knowledge. Newman's theory of education closely reflects his theory of knowledge: the whole mind, not just one aspect of the mind, has to be developed and formed. He warns that just as "some member or organ of the body may be inordinately used and developed, so may memory, or imagination, or the reasoning faculty." And "*this*," he insists, "is not intellectual culture." But rather, "as the body may be tended, cherished, and exercised with a simple view to its general health, so may the intellect also be generally exercised in order to its perfect state; and this *is* its cultivation." After all, the mind can only be logical so far as imagination and memory enable it to exercise its logical powers. Similarly, without the element of evaluation and "judgement" it is hard to see how the mind can reach decisions, however clear and lucid it may be in its thought-processes.

When it comes to the actual subjects taught in a university, Newman is again insistent on the integrity and wholeness of the intellect. His famous principle is that a university must "profess all branches of knowledge" (*Idea*, 33). But clearly this is intended as an ideal norm, as in practice no university can fulfil such a profession. But the profession is important because of the implied negative prohibition against discriminating against any particular branches of knowledge. For such discrimination involves a less than whole view of the capacity and range of the human mind. "For instance," he writes, "are we to limit our idea of University Knowledge by the evidence of our senses? then we exclude ethics; by intuition? we exclude history; by testimony? we exclude metaphysics; by abstract reasoning? we exclude physics" (*Idea*, 38). Instead, the wholeness and unity of the human mind points to the wholeness and unity of human knowledge:

> All that exist, as contemplated by the human mind, forms one large system or complex fact, and this of course resolves itself into an indefinite number of particular facts, which, as being portions of a whole, have countless relations of every kind, one towards another. Knowledge is the apprehension of these facts, whether in themselves, or in their mutual positions and bearings. And, as all taken together form one integral subject for contemplation, so there are no natural or real limits between part and part; one is ever running into another; all, as viewed by the mind, are combined together, and possess a correlative character one with another. (*Idea*, 52)

IV. Newman as Preacher

It is Newman's preoccupation with the mind that more than anything else makes him one of the most powerful preachers of all time. His Anglican sermons constitute one of the great classics of Christian spirituality if only because of the uniquely pure form of Christianity which characterizes them and which stems from their dependence on scriptural and patristic sources. But it is their homiletic art, as opposed to their theology, that I should like briefly to touch on, for it displays the profound psychological insight that we might expect from a phenomenologist of Newman's penetration and subtlety.

One of his congregation, the historian James Anthony Froude, recalled how in his preaching Newman "seemed to be addressing the most secret consciousness of each of us - as the eyes of a portrait appear to look at every person in a room."[5] But his insight was as intellectually searching as it was psychological, and nowhere more so than in his remarkable sense of the crucial part played by that inconsistency in the moral life which lurks insidiously in the very midst of apparent consistency.

> If we look to some of the most eminent saints of Scripture, we shall find their recorded errors to have occurred in those parts of their duty in which each had most trial, and generally showed obedience most perfect. *Faithful* Abraham through want of faith denied his wife. Moses, the *meekest* of men, was excluded from the land of promise for a passionate word. The *wisdom* of Solomon was reduced to bow down to idols. Barnabas again, the *son of consolation*, had a sharp contention with St. Paul. (*PS*, I, 46-47)

Newman has a penetrating diagnosis of much apparently involuntary inconsistency: to the "single or forgotten sins" of our past life are "to be traced the strange inconsistencies of character which we often witness in our experience of life. I mean, you meet continually with men possessed of a number of good points, amiable and excellent men, yet in one respect perhaps strangely perverted" (*PS*, IV, 42-43).

The severity of Newman's preaching has often been attributed to his early Calvinistic Evangelicalism, but in fact is to a very large extent due to an unremitting psychological realism: "Thus do past years rise up against us in present offences; gross inconsistencies show themselves in our character; and much need have we continually to implore God to forgive us our past transgressions, which still live in spite of our repentance, and act of themselves vigorously against our better mind, feebly influenced by that younger principle of faith, by which we fight against them" (*PS*, I, 90). On the other hand it is precisely this kind of introspective analysis which reminds us that Newman himself had once rigorously practiced the spiritual self-examination so encouraged by such standard Evangelical guides as William Wilberforce's *Practical View* (1797) and Hannah More's *Practical Piety* (1811). It may also remind us of the moral explorations of one of the greatest English novelists, George Eliot, herself a former evangelical, whose keen insight into intention and motive, and especially self-deception, raised the delineation of character in the novel to an altogether new level. This warning, for example, of the preacher that to some extent self-knowledge is impossible because it is not possible to foresee the developments of sin might equally have some from the creator of *Middlemarch*'s Mr. Bulstrode: "When a man begins to do wrong, he cannot answer for himself how far he may be carried on. He does not see beforehand, he cannot know where he shall find himself after the sin in committed. One false step forces him to another, for retreat is impossible" (*PS*, III, 67). That is why a quasi-deliberate amnesia about the sins of our past lives is so convenient, whereby people speak with "sometimes even something of tenderness and affection for their former selves; or at best they speak of themselves in a sort of moralizing way, as they might of sinners they read of, as if it were not now *their* concern what they then were" (*PS*, IV, 95). Repentance may even become psychologically impossible: "You cannot bear to be other than you are. Life would seem a blank to you, were you other" (*PS*, V, 350). Of course Newman's preaching never reaches the moral complexity and drama of George Eliot's fiction, but it can safely be said that the English sermon has never before or since shown such powerful awareness of the human psyche.

V. Newman as Writer

We have looked at Newman the philosopher, the theologian, the educator, and the preacher. It is time finally to say something of the nature of his literary achievement. Newman's genius as a satirical writer has been largely ignored, whereas it seems to me that he belongs to that great tradition of English satirists which stretches from Ben Jonson to his own contemporary, Charles Dickens. Different aspects of life provoke the laughter of contempt in different satirists; it is not very surprising to find that Newman's satire is entirely intellectual: it is only natural that the great philosopher of the mind should receive his satirical inspiration from the spectacle not of moral but of mental frailty.

His satirical art is inseparable from the fact that his writings, which were mostly occasional in origin, are the work chiefly of a supremely able controversialist, surely the greatest in the history of English literature, whose rapier-like thrusts are directed above all at the inconsistency of the opposition's arguments. I have tried to show elsewhere how closely the theme of reality and unreality, which is at the heart of Newman's thought, is connected with that of consistency and inconsistency. Nowhere is this more true than in his satirical writings where his sarcasm fastens with fascinated ferocity on the unreality of intellectual inconsistency. And this is true of both his Anglican and Catholic periods.

As a Tractarian he gleefully satirized what he saw as the inherent inconsistency of the traditional Protestant insistence on Scripture as the sole authority for faith:

We (Protestants) uphold the pure unmutilated Scripture; the Bible, and the Bible only, is the religion of Protestants; the

Bible and our own sense of the Bible. We claim a sort of
parliamentary privilege to interpret laws in our own way, and
not to suffer an appeal to any court beyond ourselves. We
know, and we view it with consternation, that all Antiquity
runs counter to our interpretation; and therefore, alas, the
Church was corrupt from *very* early times indeed. But mind,
we hold all this in a truly Catholic spirit, not in bigotry. We
allow in others the right of private judgement, and confess that
we, as others are fallible men. We confess facts are against
us; we do but claim the liberty of theorizing in spite of them.
Far be it from us to say that we are certainly right; we only
say that the whole early Church was certainly wrong. We do
not impose our belief on any one; we only say that those who
take the contrary side are Papists, firebrands, persecutors,
madmen, zealots, bigots, and an insult to the nineteenth
century. (*HS*, I, 420-21)

Newman seizes on Protestant hostility to conversions to Roman
Catholicism as the proof that the principle of so-called "private
judgement" is itself self-contradictory. Does it not prove that
"this great people is not such a conscientious supporter of the
sacred right of 'Private Judgement' as a good Protestant would
desire?" And he enjoys ridiculing an apparently glaring
inconsistency in an exuberantly comic passage:

Is it not sheer wantonness and cruelty in Baptist, Independent,
Irvingite, Wesleyan, Establishment-man, Jumper, and
Mormonite, to delight in trampling on and crushing these
manifestations of their own pure and precious charter, instead
of dutifully and reverently exalting, at Bethel, or at Dan, each
instance of it, as it occurs, to the gaze of its professing
votaries? If a staunch Protestant's daughter turns Roman, and
betakes herself to a convent, why does he not exult in the
occurrence? Why does he not give a public breakfast, or hold
a meeting, or erect a memorial, or write a pamphlet in honour
of her, and of the great undying principle she has so gloriously
vindicated? Why is he in this base, disloyal style muttering
about priests, and Jesuits, and the horrors of nunneries, in
solution to the phenomenon, when he has the fair and ample

form of Private Judgement rising before his eyes, and pleading with him. . . . All this would lead us to suspect that the doctrine of private judgement, in its simplicity, purity, and integrity, - private judgement, all private judgement, and nothing but private judgement - is held by very few persons indeed; and that the great mass of the population are either stark unbelievers in it, or deplorably dark about it; and that even the minority who are in a manner faithful to it, have glossed and corrupted the true sense of it by a miserably faulty reading, and hold, not the right of private judgement, but the private right of judgement; in other words, their own private right, and no one else's. (*Ess.*, II, 339-41)

The only sustained work of satire that Newman wrote as an Anglican is the *Tamworth Reading Room*, which consists of a series of brilliantly written letters published in *The Times* in February 1841 attacking the inconsistency of utilitarian attempts to replace religion with education. It is doubtful if Newman ever wrote anything more searingly sarcastic than when he denounced the illogicality involved in refusing to accept that "To know is one thing, to do is another."

That the mind is changed by a discovery, or saved by a diversion, and can thus be amused into immortality - that grief, anger, cowardice, self-conceit, pride, or passion can be subdued by an examination of shells or grasses, or inhaling of gases, or chipping of rocks, or calculating the longitude, is the veriest of pretences which sophist or mountebank ever professed to a gaping auditory. If virtue be a mastery over the mind, if its end be action, if its perfection be inward order, harmony, and peace, we must seek it in graver and holier places than in Libraries and Reading-rooms.

Newman later thought that he had never written with greater verve than when he ridiculed this attempt to bridge the logically unbridgeable gap between knowledge and virtue: when "was a choleric temperament ever brought under by a scientific King Canute planting his professor's chair before the rising waves"?

As for the "attempt to make man moral and religious by Libraries and Museums, let us in consistency take chemists for our cooks, and mineralogists for our masons" (*DA*, 262, 267, 268, 296).

Newman's first novel *Loss and Gain*, the first of his Catholic books, opened his most creative period as a satirist. The lack of doctrinal consistency in the Anglican position is at the heart of the story, but not content with satirizing apparent inconsistencies Newman now satirizes the very principle of inconsistency in one of the funniest passages he ever wrote:

> Our Church admitted of great liberty of thought within her pale. Even our greatest divines differed from each other in many respects; nay, Bishop Taylor differed from himself. It was a great principle in the English Church. Her true children agree to differ. In truth, there is that robust, masculine, noble independence in the English mind, which refuses to be tied down to artificial shapes, but is like, I will say, some great and beautiful production of nature - a tree, which is rich in foliage and fantastic in limb, no sickly denizen of the hothouse, or helpless dependent of the garden wall, but in careless magnificence sheds its fruits upon the free earth, for the bird of the air and the beast of the field, and all sorts of cattle, to eat thereof and rejoice. (*LG*, 84-5)

In the first of the two major satirical writings of the Catholic period, *Lectures on Certain Difficulties Felt by Anglicans in Submitting to the Catholic Church*, Newman satirizes the inherent inconsistency of the Anglo-Catholic position which he had once himself believed in. Indeed, he had been one of those Anglo-Catholic theologians whose appeal to the primitive authority of the Fathers was fraught with inconsistency.

> There they found a haven of rest; thence they looked out upon the troubled surge of human opinion and upon the crazy vessels which were labouring, without chart or compass, upon it. Judge then of their dismay, when . . . on their striking their anchors into the supposed soil, lighting their fires on it, and

fixing in it the poles of their tents, suddenly their island began to move, to heave, to splash, to frisk to and fro, to dive, and at last to swim away, spouting out inhospitable jets of water upon the credulous mariners who had made it their home.

It was the very same theologians who appealed to antiquity who also incongruously produced their "new edition of the Catholic faith, different from that held in any existing body of Christians anywhere" (*Diff.*, I, 150, 157).

Much more aggressive is the satire of *Lectures on the Present Position of Catholics*, where Newman meets head-on the virulent anti-Popery of English Protestantism. It certainly contains the best of his satirical writing and it is significant that the author himself regarded it as his "best written book" (*LD*, XXVI, 115). Again, much of the satire revolves round the inconsistency of Protestant prejudice which, just like Catholicism, rests on "*tradition* immemorial, unauthenticated *tradition.*" Far from depending solely on Scripture, Protestantism depends on the "anti-Catholic Tradition" and has a particular need "to preserve it from rush and decay, to keep it bright and keen, and ready for action in any emergency or peril." Indeed, scoffs Newman, the "Establishment is the Keeper in ordinary of those national types and blocks from which Popery is ever to be printed off." Since some facts are useful for nurturing the tradition, "preachers and declaimers" have "now a weary while been longing, and panting, and praying for some good fat scandal, one, only just one . . . to batten upon and revel in." The prejudiced Protestant is indeed ironically the child of tradition, "and, like a man who has been for a long while in one position, he is cramped and disabled, and has a difficulty and pain . . . in stretching his limbs, straightening them, and moving them freely." Again, it is no benighted Catholic country but Protestant England which "as far as religion is concerned, really must be called one large convent, or rather workhouse; the old pictures hang on the walls; the world-wide Church is chalked up on every side as a wyvern or a griffin; no pure gleam of light finds its way in or from without; the thick atmosphere refracts and distorts such struggling rays as gain admittance." Similarly, it is

> familiar to an Englishman to wonder at and to pity the recluse
> and the devotee who surround themselves with a high
> enclosure, and shut our what is on the other side of it; but was
> there ever such an instance of self-sufficient, dense, and
> religious bigotry, as that which rises up and walls in the minds
> of our fellow-countrymen from all knowledge of one of the
> most remarkable phenomena which the world has seen?
> (*Prepos.*, 43-45, 55, 74-75, 139, 178)

The fact that the "no-Popery" tradition is largely a thing of the past in England at any rate no doubt owes something to Newman himself. But what is still generally unrecognized is that the book in which with exuberant wit he sought to expose the incoherence of the tradition is itself a neglected masterpiece, which ought to be counted among the classics of English satire. And it is indeed Newman's genius as a satirical writer which perhaps more than any other aspect of his writings calls out for recognition in a centenary revaluation of his achievement.

Notes

1. John Henry Newman, *Fifteen Sermons preached before the University of Oxford.* All references are to the Longmans uniform edition (1868-81, 36 vols.) except when otherwise stated.

2. John Henry Newman, *Apologia Pro Vita Sua*, ed. Martin J. Svaglic (Oxford: Clarendon Press, 1967).

3. John Henry Newman, *Via Media*, I, xii, xciv.

4. John Henry Newman, *The Idea of a University*, ed. I. T. Ker (Oxford: Clarendon Press, 1976).

5. James Anthony Froude, *Short Studies of Great Subjects*, Fourth Series (New York: C. Scribner's Sons, 1905), 188.

2
Newman: The Man Behind the Cloud
Ronald R. Burke

Introduction

John Henry Newman was a man of considerable measure, a man of brilliance, and—as described by the postulator for the cause of his Roman Catholic canonization—*"heroicity."* The term was used by Vincent F. Blehl, S.J., who was the chairman of the Vatican's Historical Commission called to investigate the life and reputation for holiness of Cardinal Newman.[1] In 1986 he was appointed postulator for the cause, meaning he was to review the data and write the case in favor of Newman's sanctity. On August 10, 1990—the day before the centenary of Newman's death—Blehl announced that the Vatican Congregation for Sainthood had unanimously approved the "holiness" of Cardinal Newman, the immediate prelude to consideration of his canonization.

Newman is a landmark figure in both his thought and his life. As I have proposed in an earlier essay, one most remarkable thing in his thought was his exceptional ability to hold in a mutually enriching "balance" conflicting ideas from tradition and from modernity.[2] As examples of this skill, he held in balance the conflicting ideas of both permanence and development in doctrine, both certitude and probability in faith, and both assured infallibility as well as historical dependency in official papal teachings.

Such a review of Newman's ideas, however, takes the observer only the shortest possible distance into his life and personality. It offers no summary of his behavior, no insight into his compulsions and fears, no investigation of the needs and goals that shaped his decisions and development into one of the most influential figures of nineteenth century Christianity.[3] In fact, important aspects of his human personality are effectively hidden by the almost hagiographical cloud that persists even today in the most notable research into his life and works.[4]

There are in fact a number of problematic events and relationships in his life. These remain relatively unexplored and unexplained. In the brief span of this essay, I will introduce but one of those problems and then present a few words from personality theory to begin an explanation. We will introduce this problem in terms of Newman's relationship to his family. In this context, what were his goals in life? To what degree did he integrate aspects of healthy adulthood into these goals?[5] What characteristics do we see emerge in the personality of this candidate for sainthood? With an effort to maintain the "mutually-enriching balance of opposites" which was maintained in the man's own thinking, I want in this essay to explore the "shadow side" of his personality, the unconscious or preconscious thinking of John Henry Newman. Among the characteristics we will find are an aversion for the personal display of emotion and a compulsion for perfection.

I. His Relationship with His Family

John Henry Newman was born at 80 Old Broad Street in London on 21 February 1801 and was raised by his parents in the Church of England, a "Bible Religion" which consisted "not in rites or creeds, but mainly in having the bible read in Church, in the family, and in private" (GA, 43).[6] Eldest of six children, he had two brothers and three sisters. He was the "good boy" of the family, working to help his brothers and sisters in their education and to keep them in the "right kind" of faith (LD, I, 54-56). His paternal aunt, Elizabeth, and his paternal grandmother, both read the Bible to him before he could read it for himself, and he claims to have treasured the experience for

the rest of his life (*LD*, I, 251). As Charles Dessain has pointed
out, devotion to the cause of "Revealed Religion" became an
important ingredient in his entire personality and career.[7]

His father, John, was somewhat secular, with a love for
Shakespeare and for music which he received from his own
father and handed on to his son. He rose from humble beginnings
to being a rather affluent London banker—although the success
collapsed before he was fifty-five. He was rather over-bearing
in his letters to John Henry (*LD*, I, 54-56). He expressed
opposition to emotional religion and attempted to direct his son
toward a career in law.

Both parents were committed to a broad education, and
introduced their children to music and plays as well as formal
learning. Along with his younger brother, Charles, John Henry
was sent off to boarding school, at Ealing, at the time he was
seven.

All of this seems ordinary enough for the times. Yet let me
share some selective details and impressions of John Henry's
relation to his family that lead one to conclude that not
everything was entirely healthy and constructive.

Newman's father was an authority figure, requiring education
of his family and encouraging John toward law school and the
career opportunities it offered in public administration.[8] Newman
tried to prove himself to his father and to please him, but he also
rebelled against his father's detached notion of religion and the
goal of law. Communication was often not very direct between
father and son and there are few clear instances of shared
feelings. They had different goals, although they shared the
value of education as a means toward their respective goals.

There were dynamics at work here that had much to do with
shaping Newman's life and career. It was within the universe
Newman received from his parents that he had to discover what
provided resonance and meaning in terms of his own ideas and
experiences.

On 8 March 1816, as a result of the financial turmoil at the
end of the Napoleonic wars, Newman's father's bank closed its
doors. Fortunately, his partners at the bank were able to find

him a job managing a brewery in Alton, Hampshire. He failed at that job, however, and was managing another brewery, this one in Clerkenwell, by 1821. Soon after that, this man who had risen from relatively humble beginnings to considerable affluence, was crushed by the final blow of personal bankruptcy. He warned John Henry to take all his possessions out of the family house and off to Oxford before the property was sold, along with its contents, as part of the bankruptcy.

In September of 1823, at age 59, Mr. John Newman died, shortly after John Henry had returned from Oxford to be at his bedside. The younger Newman recorded that his deceased father looked "beautiful and calm," proposing that it would be difficult for anyone to be a materialist after seeing a dead body. It was characteristic of John Henry to be so philosophical, rather than explicitly emotional, even upon seeing the dead body of his own father.

Newman's relation to his siblings is filled with stories of enduring difficulties. The one for whom he expressed strongest affection was Mary, his youngest sister, and for her *especially*—if not excessively—after she died at the age of nineteen.[9] It was as if she, who had looked up to her oldest brother so much, were the safest to love, both in her youth and in her death.[10]

A friend who had been with Mary and John when she was taken suddenly sick at table, later returned to the house and described Newman just after the death:

> I felt a shock in entering the house, seeing no one but you so pale, and so calm, and yet so inwardly moved; and how, when I asked you to pray with us for her, you made a great effort to quiet your voice, sitting against the table, your eyes on the fire, and you answered, "I must tell you the truth; she is dead already."[11]

Again at this death Newman was attempting not to show emotion, struggling to quiet his voice, focusing upon "the truth," avoiding eye contact, a facade of calm and yet so pale.

Newman's two other sisters, along with their mother, lived close to him at Iffley, near Oxford, after their father's death. They depended upon his financial support. One might think that the time at Iffley would have been one of close sharing by family members especially bonded to each other. That is anything but the way that Newman recalled it. He claimed his mother and sisters did not like some of his closest friends, did not like the distinctive principles of the Oxford Movement in which he was integrally involved, and that their differences only increased as the Movement developed. On a more domestic issue, they differed with him in their attitude toward their two brothers, Frank and Charles. "They had a full right to their own views," Newman wrote, "but I did not imitate them in bearing patiently what could not be helped" (*LD*, VI, 119). There was something fundamentally wrong with the religious beliefs of the two brothers, John felt, something he could not passively tolerate. He repeatedly struggled to correct their errors.

Within one year of each other, Newman's sisters married two Mozley brothers, Harriett marrying Tom, and Jemima John. Tom Mozley was a former student of Newman's and later an Oriel Fellow. John was an older brother, a partner in the family publishing and printing business. In October of 1843, Harriett wrote to Newman a very angry letter, claiming that he was attempting to seduce her husband into Roman Catholicism. This was the last contact she ever had with him, the last letter she wrote.[12]

Newman's other sister, Jemima, remained in some communication with John Henry throughout his life. She visited him at the Birmingham Oratory for lunch in June of 1867. We do not hear anything of their conversation or of their feelings for each other, but together they played Beethoven's Sonata in A minor, Jemima on the piano and John on the violin. Newman recalled that he was so "transported" by the music that he could hardly complete the first movement. Music can be used as either a bridge to others or as a means for maintaining distance. In this instance it seems to have maintained John in distance from Jemima and provided a bridge to the sister who had died.

Newman later elaborated on how the music reminded him of Mary's young face, the nineteen-year old whose face would never change in his eyes, though she now would have been in her fifty-ninth year (*LD*, XXIII, 234, 255).

John Henry's youngest brother, Francis, was commonly referred to as a "free-thinker." John had paid for his education at Oxford, after their father's bankruptcy, with money he made by tutoring. The money seemed well-spent: Francis gained a double-first in University exams, even better than John Henry had done. As congratulations, John sent Francis a picture of the Virgin and Child, but Francis took it as an affront, a sign his brother was already a Roman Catholic. He returned it to the store.[13]

Under the leadership of Rev. Walter Mayers, the same person who had helped John in his first religious conversion, Francis had become much more of an Evangelical than John Henry ever was. He resigned from his fellowship at Balliol College because of his Nonconformist views. He left England as part of the Plymouth Brethren on a three-year Evangelical mission to convert Moslems in Persia.

Upon his brother's return to England in 1833, Newman found him to be "ultra-Protestant," thinking everyone could get "the true doctrines of the gospel for himself from the Bible" (*LD*, V, 166-67). John Henry found this view much too rational and individualistic. He sternly warned Francis that his position of individual self-sufficiency would unravel. Since Francis was leading a group of Christians, John labeled his position "an effort toward schism" (*LD*, V, 315). He was so upset that he refused to meet Francis "in a familiar way or sit at table" with him, although he said he had no objection to further (formal) discussion in person or by letter. Certainly John was placing more value upon a religious position than upon family friendship.

Seven years later, there had been some change. In a letter sent in April of 1840 to Jemima, John first apologized for the way he had treated his brother nineteen years before (!) and then expressed relief that Francis was no longer set on causing a schism in the church. Since Francis had resigned his leadership position, John decided there was no longer any reason "for separating from his society." He also explained, however, that "free unrestrained intercourse between them was impossible and that to attempt it would be a great mistake."[14] It was as if Newman knew there were long-term differences between them, differences that would emerge in "unrestrained intercourse." He chose rather to erect walls than to risk personal, intimate conversation.

For strictly human reasons, Francis had the final word in the argument between the two brothers. One year after John's death, Francis published a book, entitled *Early History of Cardinal Newman*, to explain how treacherous and evil John had been in his religious views.

With his other brother, Charles, Newman also had disputes regarding religion. In the summer of 1823, Charles defended a skepticism about the claims of Christianity. John Henry replied with the Evangelical argument that religious truth cannot be attained without the right kind of "moral seriousness and sincerity"—which may have sounded quite patronizing to a younger brother. When Charles left home after his father's death, John helped him get a job as a clerk in the Bank of England. He left the job five years later, however, and moved through a whole series of jobs. He was described by some as "becoming more and more strange and eccentric."[15] Others have compared him to a semi-lunatic, with flashes of unusual intelligence.[16] Whatever his precise character and personality, there was no special love lost between John and Charles.

Toward his mother Newman seemed to have an ambivalent, love-hate relationship. Although she was from a family of French Huguenot exiles, her religion was not a rigid Calvinism. With her husband she was a follower of the national religion of England, which focused primarily upon the Bible and the *Book of Common Prayer*. As a child, John Henry wrote to her often from school and was meticulous in choosing gifts to please her.

Yet after Newman's mother died, on 17 May 1836, his reaction was at best philosophical. He shared with Jemima, who had married three weeks before, that the death was almost like an answer to his "prayers," because he had been getting into debt and less able to support his mother. It was remarkable, he wrote, how "strangely" prayers were "answered—so much so that to pray seems to be using an edged tool" (*LD*, V, 322-23).

He went on to say that his mother "has much misunderstood my religious views. . . . In consequence, I who am conscious to myself I never thought any thing more precious than her sympathy and praise, had none of it" (*LD*, V, 313-14).

It seems Newman lamented here to his sister that he did not receive from his mother (nor from the rest of his family) the love ("sympathy and praise") that he wanted and needed. He went on to recount that because of misunderstandings between them that he had suffered much from bringing his mother to Oxford. He said he "knew in his heart" how much they loved each other, but he knew he had sometimes seemed rude to her even when she had been kind to him.

Close to the core of the fundamental perplexity expressed in this letter were the words: "I have some sort of dread and distress, which I cannot describe, of being the object of attention" (*LD*, V, 314). Here what Newman seems to express is a fear of intimacy, especially intimacy with women, intimacy in terms of the sharing of affection. In the abstract he wants it, but in particular situations he is frightened away from it.

After his mother and father had died, Newman had retained communication with only one of four surviving siblings. How did he look back upon his family relationships?

In 1845, soon after his reception into the Roman Catholic church, Newman reviewed his relationship to friends and family. Certainly it was a time of separation for him, personal and geographical, as well as familial and existential. It divided him from his previous work in the local parish, from his former Anglican colleagues, and from his long-time place of residence and prayer, the hermitage he had built at Littlemore, near Oxford. It was at this time of separation that he wrote: "So many dead, so many separated. My mother gone; my sisters nothing to me, or rather foreign to me" (*LD*, XXXI, 102).

What made his sisters—at first thought—"nothing" to him?

Why are his father and his brothers not even mentioned in this soliloquy? Does he feel he has totally left his past, including his Anglican family, in joining the Roman Catholic church? Does he feel this is in keeping with the call of Christ, or is he wanting to divorce himself from unhappy memories and flawed relationships? Were there no positive family feelings strong enough to survive this denominational separation?

In summary of his view of his relationships to people and his family, Newman himself wrote revealing words to his good friend, John Keble. He knew he was naturally "cold and reserved to people," but more important was his claim, in absolute and universal terms, that "(I) cannot ever realize to myself that any one loves me."[17] Those are the words of a very lonely person, a person calling out for love, a person who perhaps had not fully experienced the bonding and the development of trust that is appropriate to the earliest years of childhood.

Did Newman ever overcome the fear of intimacy and the absence of feeling loved?[18] Let me conclude this brief summary of family relationships and feelings with the story of what occurred at his death. He went in June of 1888 to London to meet with a lawyer and make his last will. The stipulations of that will were carried out two years later at his death. He was buried, as he had requested, in a kind of *grand* Victorian deed, on top of the grave of his "soul-friend" from Littlemore days, Ambrose St. John ("Sinjun").[19] It was as if, again, proximity and affection were safest after dead.

II. Some Notes on Personality

Personality is largely the result of the relationships a child has with its parents in its early environment. By the time a child is four or five years old, it has a separate sense of self and at least the beginnings of its lasting personality. Although the child's identity is still very fluid, everyone emerges from childhood as a unique member of a particular personality type, and his or her psychological potentials develop and deteriorate within the boundaries of that particular type.

Newman's personality type can be described in one theory, called "Enneagrams," by the number "One" (of nine possible types). Persons in this type are referred to as "Reformers."[20] Such persons are principled and orderly, striving always for perfection and sometimes punitive in their relationships. They are compulsive for the attainment of perfection in themselves and in others; they are critical of those who do not "fit" their image of perfection. They tend to sublimate their emotions in their quest for perfection. Contemporary examples include Pope John Paul II and Margaret Thatcher.

Being classified as a "Reformer" does not mean that an individual is any more or less healthy than anyone else in the population. Each of the nine types in the Enneagrams has its own distinctive collection of compulsions and aversions. Newman, as a "Reformer," was healthy in many ways, but did have, like all of us, his own particular struggle with complexities of human personality.

According to the theory, Newman became a "Reformer" by identifying negatively with his father in early childhood. This negative orientation encouraged the development of Newman's superego: he internalized a fear of condemnation and sought to avoid it by being blameless. The message playing continuously in his head was something like: "You are not acceptable as you are; you must be better, always better."

In a sense, Newman's superego did not allow him to be a child. He was forced to be an "adult" by the time he left for Ealing. He feared being punished for impulsiveness, selfishness, or pleasure—all parts of the natural behavior of a young child. He learned to repress his emotions and other "childish" impulses. Because of this situation, he distanced himself from his father and decided not to be like him. To avoid being condemned, he would have to be better than his father.

Like all Ones, Newman grew up with the notion that unless he was perfect he was not acceptable. This can overdo the value of perfection. But that is exactly what Newman did throughout his life: demand a particular kind of perfection, a perfection he eventually based upon the ideal of the early church. This quest for perfection sometimes led him to dissatisfaction and anger with himself, with his family, and with his surroundings.

> Not content to be as they are (according to the Enneagram theory), Ones feel the obligation to be better. They must somehow rise higher, beyond human nature into the realm of the Absolute.[21]

Newman combined this compulsion for perfection with a particular mission in the world: promoting and correcting the revealed religion of Christianity. To this goal he sublimated almost all his emotions, even before some of them, like affection and intimacy, were substantially developed. In face-to-face, interpersonal, relations, the one emotion with which he was most confident was the expression of (refined) anger. His tempered anger was often directed at those he thought were not living up to his early-church ideal of Christian perfection.

Recognition of this personality type helps us to understand some of the most famous words from Newman's *Apologia*. There he retells the story of his conversion at fifteen years of age. He tells how evangelicalism retrieved some thoughts and experiences from early in his life, especially the dream that he was actually an angel and the material world an illusion. In the heart of the fifteen-year old's five-month conversion experience (from the August 1 conclusion of summer term, to the December 21 conclusion of Fall term) he came to "rest in the thought of two and two only absolute and luminously self-evident beings, myself and my Creator."

This conclusion is interesting both for what it includes and what it excludes. To explain what it includes, it is important to remember that morality and conscience were always an integral part of Newman's youth,[22] from the time Bible stories were being read to him to the time at fifteen when he read Paine, Hume, and Voltaire at Ealing and suggested to his father that he might want to be moral without being religious. He was not sure there was a necessary place for God, but morality was necessary.

In the new power of analysis and abstraction he was obtaining at his conversion, he had a new perspective upon his commitment to morality. He realized that his intense reflection upon moral action itself guaranteed the reality of the moral agent, himself. It also guaranteed to him that there was some Ideal, a Perfect, a Judge, a Norm for that morality.[23] With the influence of his Evangelical tutor, Rev. Walter Mayers, he saw that this Norm in fact was the God of Revealed Religion. The pieces of the puzzle fit, pieces from childhood and from young adulthood. They connected his recent analysis and reflection with the early and influential experiences of Bible and Catechism reading in his home.

There was a differentiating and developmental side to this conclusion as well. Who is excluded by the "myself and my Creator"? This emotional and intellectual break-through was a confirmation of independence. Newman was differentiating himself from his father, the previous law-giver and moral "enforcer" in his world. John Henry was taking responsibility upon himself and his God. This step gave him the power to stand more strongly against his parents' wishes. Hence he was able to choose a more Evangelical form of Anglicanism. In the same year he also made a preliminary choice for celibacy, rather than intending the grandchildren his parents requested. Similarly, he later chose ordination rather than law, chose a leadership role in the Oxford Movement, and chose Roman Catholicism rather than the Anglican church.

Conclusion

In this selective view of Newman's relation to his family, what have we seen? We have seen a man who came to be quite seriously separated from his parents and siblings. The separation reflects the shadow of a personality and its potential problems. Newman had a proclivity for an angry and excessive drive to fulfill a particular vision of perfection. He also had the potential for the excessive repression of emotions. These are propensities that Reformers need to struggle with throughout their lives.

As a young adult, Newman was dedicated to his family's welfare. This dedication was directed by a particular vision of perfection, toward a particular kind of "right religion." Newman saw himself as the "expert" on what this right religion required. He often disagreed with his family regarding this religion, and was quite upset when they disagreed with him. His dedication seemed to transcend personal choice. It constituted a compulsion and led Newman onto a lonely, critical path. The path was not one of pride, vanity, or self-will. It was a compulsion for perfection, a perfection rooted in the church of early Christianity.

Another side of Newman we have seen is in his "dread and distress," his repression/avoidance of emotion and affection. He had an enormous number of friends.[24] He had the capacity for profound feelings. Yet he felt alone and could not believe that he was truly loved. His capacity for feelings showed itself primarily in the abstract, in the safety and isolation of letters and of remembering, not in face-to-face encounters. In relating to adults he consistently buried feelings under a philosophical demeanor. Even in letters he often was unable to share what he later admitted he actually had felt. He had an aversion to the "excessive" display of emotions.

What does all of this say regarding Newman's heroicity and his candidacy for canonization? It does not constitute so much the detection of flaws as it does a perception of the whole man. His drive for perfection and his avoidance of emotions does tend more toward world-denunciation than toward world-celebration. This places Newman in a particular Roman Catholic tradition of holiness. The tradition predates Christianity, parallels a tradition of Stoicism, and has been "Christianized" in monasteries and desert monks since the second century. Let there be no doubt: this man was a great human being. His was an effort toward perfection which employed the personality that was father to the man. His personality did not exemplify every dimension of maturity and health. Yet it can also exemplify maturity and be replete with health. Newman was in many ways—and in the eyes of so many people—selfless, objective and inspirational, with a personality of intensity, integrity, and completeness.

Notes

1. See Vincent F. Blehl's "Prelude to the Making of a Saint," *America* vol. 160, no. 9 (March 11, 1989), 213–16.

2. Ronald Burke, "Newman, Lindbeck, and Models of Doctrine," delivered at the Creighton University Newman Centenary, October 18–20, 1990.

3. As a catalyst for some of the ideas in this paper, I am indebted to conversation with Edward J. Miller from the College of New Rochelle. One of the most insightful and succinct explorations of Newman's personality is provided by Jan-Hendrik Walgrave in his *Newman the Theologian* (London: Geoffrey Chapman, 1960), 21–25.

4. From the vast amount of material available for the review of Newman's life, I have used primarily: (1) *The Letters and Diaries of John Henry Newman*, ed. Charles Stephen Dessain, et al. (2) *John Henry Newman: Autobiographical Writings*, ed. Henry Tristram (New York: Sheed and Ward, 1957). (3) John Henry Newman, *Apologia Pro Vita Sua*, 1864 (London: Longmans, Green, 1947). I have also used four biographies: (1) Charles Stephen Dessain, *John Henry Newman*, second edition (Stanford, CA: Stanford University Press, 1971). (2) Wilfrid Ward, *The Life of John Henry Cardinal Newman*, 2 vols. (London: Longmans, Green, 1913). (3) Ian Ker, *John Henry Newman: A Biography* (Oxford: Clarendon Press, 1988). (4) Louis Bouyer, *Newman: His Life and Spirituality* (New York: P. J. Kenedy and Sons, 1958). Each of these has strengths, but none gets deeply enough into Newman's personality and the dynamics of his development.

5. In addition to his relationship to his family, it would be valuable to explore further his relationship to his companions at Littlemore, to women in his life such as Maria Giberne, and his

relation to members of the Oratory. Particular events in his young-adult life that are in need of explanation include his first experience of conversion, his relatively poor showing on his university graduation exams, and his argument with his college provost.

6. This is Newman's own description of his family's "Bible Religion" in John Henry Newman, *An Essay in Aid of a Grammar of Assent*, Longman's uniform edition.

7. In his outstanding introduction to Newman's life and thought, Dessain explains that Newman was led to accept "Revealed Religion" whole-heartedly as a boy and then chose to seek out its full and balanced content in his life. This devotion, Dessain claims, gave his life its unity and purpose. It led him to oppose secular control of the Church of England, to join the Roman Church, and to seek remedy for the various deficiencies he found even there (*John Henry Newman*, xii).

8. For notes on Newman's father wanting for his son the career in law, see Fr. Zeno, O.F.M., *Newman's Inner Life* (San Francisco: Ignatius Press, 1987, orig. 1952), 29–30. In 1819 young Newman did join a pre-law club at Lincoln's Inn (*LD*, I, 69). I propose that he soon knew, however, that he did not *want* a career in law. Consciously or unconsciously, he *intended* to do *so poorly* on his University exams (only passing, not getting a first or second) that he did *not qualify* for the career in law. This gave an incontrovertible answer to his father's desire. In comparison to other exams he took at Oxford, before and after, this one stands out as an aberration. He wrote home quite content about the outcome shortly after the results were posted. The excuses offered by other scholars (that the exam was given sooner than expected and that the college had not given him all the guidance that he needed) seem inadequate to explain the data.

9. I am reminded of words by Walgrave regarding Newman's fear of loving material reality. "Consider his ambiguous attitude towards the beauties of nature. When he encounters them directly by the contact of sense, he invariably feels ill at ease, unresponsive; but no sooner are they presented indirectly, interiorly, in memory, than they move him to ecstasy" (*Newman*

the Theologian, 19).

10. To read someone who is *not* making the point that Newman's affection for Mary was excessive, but emphasizes that it was unique and extremely important in his life, see the lengthy treatment in Bouyer (*Newman: His Life and Spirituality*, 102–15).

11. Letter from Maria Giberne, in *Letters and Correspondence of John Henry Newman during his Life in the English Church*, ed. Anne Mozley, 2 vols. (London: Longmans, Green, 1891), 1, 115.

12. Forty-seven years later Harriett's only child, Grace Langford, who hadn't seen Newman since she was three years old, came to visit her uncle on a trip to England from Australia, where she had moved with her husband. Two days after their meeting her uncle died (Ker, *John Henry Newman: A Biography*, 745).

13. Bouyer, *Newman: His Life and Spirituality*, 82–83.

14. Unpublished letter to Mrs. J. Mozley, 10 April 1840, quoted by Ker, *John Henry Newman: A Biography*, 199.

15. Ker, *John Henry Newman: A Biography*, 106.

16. Bouyer, *Newman: His Life and Spirituality*, 83.

17. "Consider, too, his seeming 'egocentricity', because of which his heart, so sensitive and hungry for friendship, could never give itself completely; hence his continual, painful sense of isolation" (Walgrave, *Newman the Theologian*, 20).

18. *LD*, VI, 119. Newman received vast numbers of letters offering praise for his example and thanks for his guidance as a spiritual director (see Blehl, "Prelude to the Making of a Saint"). None of these letters seem to have given Newman the sense that he was loved.

19. Ker, *John Henry Newman: A Biography*, 745.

20. The enneagram theory was made known in Paris in the 1920's by George Ivanovitch Gurdjieff (1877–1949). It came to the United States by way of Chile with the help of Oscar Ichaso, founder of the Arica Institute, in 1971. It was used at Jesuit theological centers for religious growth beginning in the early 1970's. It has parallels to theories by Freud, Jung, and Karen Horney, but is extraordinary in the detail it offers regarding its

types and their particular trajectories toward sickness and toward health. See J. G. Bennett, *Enneagram Studies* (York Beach, Me: Samuel Weiser Press, 1983) and Don Richard Riso, *Personality Types: Using the Enneagram for Self-Discovery* (Boston: Houghton Mifflin Company, 1987).

21. Riso, *Personality Types*, 275.

22. For the importance of conscience in Newman's life, see Walgrave, *Newman the Theologian*, 22–25.

23. See Walgrave's comments on this: "For him, God was the Judge to come, whom he awaited with anxious foreboding. His own greatest concern was to prepare himself for the judgment by a rigorous obedience and a continuous moral purification. Only the absolutely pure could sustain the presence of the God of sanctity. . . (His) interior life (was) ruled by this fear and foreboding. . . This fear of God forms, then, the inmost spring of his life" (*Newman the Theologian*, 20–22).

24. Stories of his facility for friendship abound: from the walls lined with photographs of friends which surrounded his altar at the Birmingham Oratory (to remember them at Mass) to the thousands of letters received in praise at the time of his death. Some knew him "to shed cheerfulness as a sunbeam sheds lights, even when many difficulties were pressing." Others recall that he was "'unserious', natural, energetic, humorous, and practical." Yet my reading of so many letters and accounts finds him always to operate at one stage removed, in a world of only two luminous beings, God and himself. Others were always a step away, not fully trusted, or perhaps not fully real. Even if a loneliness of leadership, this was an aloneness nonetheless.

3

The Androgynous Ideal: Newman's *Callista*
Joseph H. Wessling

I

With the publication in 1973 of Carolyn Heilbrun's *Toward a Recognition of Androgyny*,[1] the androgynous ideal became a subject of much discussion among literary scholars. Though any precise, detailed description of the androgynous personality immediately becomes debatable, it is generally agreed that such a person would be an optimum blend or fusion of characteristics traditionally identified as either masculine or feminine, and that, so far as *psychological* traits are concerned, there is no masculine ideal distinct from a feminine ideal. For Heilbrun, the terms *masculine* and *feminine* are "little more than unexamined, received ideas," and she goes on to present a short catalogue of such assumptions.

> According to the conventional view, "masculine" equals forceful, competent, competitive, controlling, vigorous, unsentimental, and occasionally violent; "feminine" equals tender, genteel, intuitive rather than rational, passive, unaggressive, readily given to submission.[2]

The list is, of course, subject to modification or expansion, and Heilbrun herself strays from it elsewhere without contradiction, but her point is well made, and her book has provided the impetus for further theorizing and literary analysis.

Contemporary resistance to the androgynous ideal Heilbrun traces to the patriarchy of the Judeo-Christian tradition and to the legacy of Victorianism:

Yet in the matter of sexual polarization and the rejection of androgyny we still accept the convictions of Victorianism; we view everything, from our study of animal habits to our reading of literature, through the paternalistic eyes of the Victorian era.

Masculine domination of life accompanied by extreme sexual polarization was not, of course, unique to the nineteenth century. Patriarchy reached its apotheosis in the years of Victoria's reign, but it is a habit thousands of years old, its roots deep in the Judeo-Christian tradition.[3]

Much of Heilbrun's book is devoted to a discussion of writers who, in spite of traditional attitudes, either advocated an androgynous ideal (as did Coleridge) or realized this ideal imaginatively (as did Shakespeare and George Eliot). It is significant but understandable that John Henry Newman should have been omitted from Heilbrun's discussion of androgynous minds, as he has been omitted from discussions of androgyny in general. No discussion can be all-inclusive, and Newman's fullest realization of the androgynous ideal, *Callista: A Sketch of the Third Century*,[4] is a novel few are expected to have read.

II

That the androgynous vision should be found in Newman is ironic as well as significant. He has an important place in the Victorian age and in the Judeo-Christian tradition, both of which are cited by Heilbrun as roots of the contemporary resistance to androgyny. Secondly, he played increasingly prominent roles first in the Anglican then in the Roman Catholic Church—both highly patriarchal institutions. Thirdly, though he praised his otherwise "unhappy age" for providing so many opportunities for women,[5] he spoke out for "institutions which give dignity and independence to the position of women in society,"[6] and chided the Tamworth Reading Room for admitting only "virtuous women,"[7] he was not an advocate of radical reform either in the Church or in society at large. Therefore, that the androgynous ideal should be advanced in the works of John Henry Newman may come as a surprise even to some who know that the famous convert came close to realizing this ideal in his own person.

At this point, it should be acknowledged that Newman did not set forth a *theory* of androgyny, nor did he use that word to denote a fully developed personality. The subject of androgyny was not one of his formal undertakings, and I do not presume to speculate what the result might have been had he done so. However, in *The Idea of a University*,[8] Newman sets forth a portrait of the "gentleman" in which he anticipates the ideal blend of "masculine" and "feminine" characteristics discussed by Heilbrun over a century later. Newman's gentleman is humanely "forceful, competent" and "controlling" when occasion requires (*forcible* and *decisive* are Newman's terms (*Idea*, 160), but the male excesses of "competitive, . . . unsentimental, and occasionally violent" he does not allow: "It is almost a definition of a gentleman to say he is one who never inflicts pain . . . he is tender towards the bashful, gentle towards the distant, and merciful towards the absurd" (*Idea*, 159). Most striking of all in Newman's portrait are the words "a certain gentleness and effeminacy of feeling, which is the attendant on civilization" (*Idea*, 160). It is striking, not only because of the word *effeminacy*, clearly implying that a man has a feminine side and that its development is necessary to his wholeness. It is striking also because this androgynous personality is not just an individual goal but a need of society. Thus Newman anticipates Heilbrun's observation that "the connection between civilization and androgyny is close."[9]

There is, of course, a striking limitation in the lectures which comprise *The Idea of a University*. They are concerned with the education of young *men* only. Liberal education produces the "gentleman," and "it is well to be a gentleman" (*Idea*, 91). The development of young women falls outside the concern of those 1852 lectures, but perhaps not outside the concern of Newman, who during the same period of his life produced *Callista*, begun in 1848, set aside, and completed in 1855. *Callista*, though rightly ranked well below *The Idea of a University*, both as an

aesthetic and as an intellectual achievement, nonetheless moves
beyond the latter's androgynous vision in two important ways:
the androgynous ideal is realized in woman as well as in man,
and the androgynous ideal is specifically associated with the
Christian faith.

III

Callista is set in the city of Sicca, near Carthage, at the onset
of the Decian persecution (250 c.e.). The reader is first introduced, not to the title character, but to Agellius, the twenty-two-
year-old assistant bailiff (or overseer) of a large farm. His father
Strabo, an ex-soldier and convert to Christianity died when the
boy was eight years old, and Agellius and his brother Juba were
raised by their pagan uncle Jucundus. Agellius has persevered
in the Christian faith, and, because he is gentle, even indulgent,
with the workers and because he shuns pagan orgies, he is ridiculed for his lack of manliness. The severe, unsentimental
bailiff Vitricus attributes his softness to Christianity (*Call.*, 8) as
does ten-year-old Firmian, who belittles him as one of those
"lacadaisical folk who bear insults tamely" (*Call.*, 159). Among
those who jeer is Juba, "a tall, swarthy, wild-looking youth"
(*Call.*, 24)—an Esau-type. He seems "as free from feeling of any
kind, from what is called *heart*, as if he had been a stone" (*Call.*,
26). He prides himself on his "logical head" (*Call.*, 26) and upon
being "my own master" (*Call.*, 27). Juba taunts Agellius for not
having "the pluck to be a Christian" (*Call.*, 28) and accuses him
of not believing "a bit more about religion than I do" (*Call.*, 29).
Unlike Vitricus, who urges Agellius to partake in the pagan
orgies, Juba is contemptuous of the animalistic revelers but con-
siders his brother's refusal to be a spectator "unmanly" (*Call.*,
27). Juba, in short, makes his first appearance in the novel as the
anti-androgynous male: competitive, unsentimental, proud of his
logical mind, and (in his own view) self-controlled; his contempt
for the androgynous character of Christians is shown in his em-
barrassment for having in a moment of "weakness" almost sub-
mitted to baptism because the old bishop "said some *womanish*

words to me" (*Call.*, 26, emphasis added). Juba will eventually experience conversion, but only after his pride has been undermined by demonic possession and subsequently by a temporary loss of his mental faculties.

Jucundus, one of the more fully realized characters in the novel, is not a macho male like his nephew Juba. He is good-natured, positive, and warmly attached to the reigning paganism. His philosophy of life is *carpe diem*: "All is vanity but eating and drinking . . . Life is short" (*Call.*, 49). Though he has no sympathy for the abstract Christian, he becomes actively concerned when the target of persecution is someone dear to him, intervening successfully to save Agellius, unsuccessfully on behalf of Callista. If Jucundus falls short of the androgynous ideal—and he does—it is chiefly in his addiction to the pragmatic and rational. Roman religion is to be adhered to, not because one believes in the gods, but because the unity of the state is thereby served. Adherence to any religion out of passionate devotion is fanaticism.

Jucundus, being a prosperous retailer of small idols, charms, and other pagan objects has engaged two young Greek artists, brother and sister, to supply him with merchandise. Both Aristo and Callista have been nurtured in Greek philosophy and are adherents of no religion. Callista, however, has been so edified by the death of her Christian slave Chione that she longs to know more about the Christian God. She has "the calm of Greek sculpture" though "the expression on her face was most feminine"; she is possessed of a "strong will," has "no appearance of timidity in her manner; very little of modesty, and has seldom lost her self-possession" (*Call.*, 167–68). Callista's "masculine" side is thus clearly well developed. On the other hand, when she loves someone, her devotion can approach subservience, as it has with Aristo, who observes,

> She loved me so much, she never grudged me anything; . . .
> She wished to stay in Greece, but she came to this detestable
> Africa all for me. She would be bright and gay when I would
> have her so. She had no will of her own. (*Call.*, 222)

One should not mistake this devotion for weakness. Callista, even before conversion, comes close to an androgynous ideal. She may sacrifice her preferences out of love, but her principles and convictions are another matter. When Agellius comes to her as a suitor, she rejects him, against the advice of Aristo. Though she is not yet a Christian, Agellius is too tepid a Christian to be acceptable. He speaks of himself rather than of his God; he seeks his happiness in her rather than in God, she charges.

It is immediately after Callista's rejection of Agellius that the Decian persecution comes to Sicca, intensified by a plague of locusts, which is blamed upon the Christians. When Callista goes to Agellius's home to warn him, she finds, not Agellius, but one Caecilius—later identified as Cyprian, the exiled bishop of Carthage—and Caecilius unfolds to her the story and teachings of Christianity. Callista does not convert, finding Christianity "too beautiful to be anything else than a dream" (*Call.*, 170). But she recognizes in this priest who shall be the instrument of her conversion, an androgynous personality: "There was a gentleness and a tenderness mingled with your strength which was new to me. I said, Here at last is a god" (*Call.*, 176). But Caecilius assures her that he is not a god but a sinful man, and so her quest goes on.

This conversation is interrupted by the approach of a mob. Caecilius is seized, but freed through the trickery of Juba. Callista is carried off as an accused Christian, and, though she protests she is nothing of the kind, she cannot bring herself to offer incense upon the altar of Jupiter.

In a scene that would be comic except for the grimness of the situation, Aristo attempts to restore his sister to her senses and thus to save her life. He brings to her prison cell Sicca's leading philosopher and teacher, Polemo, a pompous celebrity, a name-dropper, ostentatious in manners and dress, who has himself carried about Sicca on a litter. He is a caricature of rational man and an unabashed male chauvinist, telling Callista that "There had always been women above the standard of their sex, and they had ever held converse with men of mind" (*Call.*, 240). To this insult he adds sophistry: burning incense upon the altar of Jupiter means "nothing else than that you are loyal to Roman power" (*Call.*, 241). And the sophistry reaches a crescendo in what follows:

> I love Greece, but I love truth better; and I look at facts, I grasp them, and I confess to them. The whole earth, through untold centuries, has at length grown into the imperial dominion of Rome. It has converged and coalesced in all its various parts into one Rome. This, which we see, is the last, the perfect state of human society. The course of things, the force of natural powers, as is well understood by all great lawyers and philosophers, cannot go further. Unity has come at length, and unity is eternity. It will be for ever, because it is one. The principle of dissolution is eliminated. (*Call.*, 241–42)

Polemo's rationalism is as ineffectual with Callista as is his snob appeal:

> Blush, blush, Grecian Callista, you with a glorious nationality of your own to go shares with some hundred peasants, slaves, thieves, beggars, hucksters, tinkers, cobblers, and fishermen! A lady of high character, of brilliant accomplishments, to be the associate of the outcasts of society! (*Call.*, 243)

Polemo assures Callista that he believes in God—in "one, eternal, self-existing something." To which Callista replies,

> I feel that God within my heart. I feel myself in his presence. He says to me 'Do this; don't do that.' . . . So you see, Polemo, I believe in what is more than a mere 'something:' . . . That speaker I love and fear . . . I sacrifice to him alone. (*Call.*, 244–45)

Polemo leaves in disgust—the male principle of dispassionate logic having failed in its task. Aristo's one further effort to save his sister, at least from prolonged torture, reflects the male code of honor: he sends her a dagger that she may die "nobly" (*Call.*, 278).

Callista is not at this point a Christian, but she is ripe for conversion. She had failed to convert in her first meeting with Caecilius because, although she was taken with his androgynous person and the beauty of his teaching, the Christian God had not yet become a reality to her. Now, in prison, she reads the gospel of Luke, and the androgynous God, whom she saw mirrored in Caecilius, takes on reality in Jesus Christ. Her subsequent baptism by Caecilius, who has managed to visit her, is followed by a vision which is central to Newman's androgynous motif. Callista is transported in dream to "her own native Greece, more sunny and bright than before." At first she wanders alone through an uninhabited landscape. But suddenly there is music and fragrance and a heavenly glory.

> And there came out of the grottos and glens and woods, and out of the seas, myriads of bright images, whose forms she could not discern; and these came all around her, . . . And as she gazed, she thought she saw before her a well-known face, only glorified. She, who had been a slave, now was arrayed more brilliantly than an oriental queen; . . . And as she looked more earnestly, . . . the face changed, and now was more marvelous still. It had an innocence in its look, and also a tenderness, which bespoke both Maid and Mother, and so transported Callista, that she must needs advance towards her, out of love and reverence. (*Call.*, 275)

Callista approaches the figure, dancing and singing. Then there is a fresh change in the image.

> The light of Divinity now seems to beam through (the features), and the hair parted, and hung down on each side of the forehead; and there was a crown of another fashion from the Lady's round about it, made of what looked like thorns. And the palms of the hands were spread out as if towards her, and there were marks of wounds in them. And the vestment had fallen, and there was a deep opening in the side. And as she stood entranced before Him, and motionless, she felt a consciousness that her own palms were pierced like His, and

her feet also. And she looked round, and saw the likeness of
His face and of His wounds upon that whole company. (*Call.*,
275–76)

Callista's glorified slave Chione evolves into the Heavenly
Queen, who evolves into the supremely androgynous figure of
Christ. Callista's vision—indeed Newman's novel—may be
viewed as a gloss on Paul's words to the Galatians:

As many of you as were baptized into Christ have clothed
yourselves with Christ. There is no longer Jew or Greek, there
is no longer slave or free, there is no longer male and female;
for all of you are one in Christ Jesus.[10]

For Newman, oneness in Christ is more than equality of the
sexes; it is a participation in His androgynous Being. Such is the
state of Caecilius when we first meet him, of Callista through
conversion, and eventually of a strengthened Agellius, if we
accept Newman's speculation that he is the same Agellius who
later suffered martyrdom as the Bishop of Sicca.

Androgynous development can occur apart from Christianity
as in Newman's gentleman, who may well be an unbeliever
(*Idea*, 160). But can the fullness of Christian sainthood be non-
androgynous? The implication of *Callista* is that full union with
Christ comes only to those who are tender as well as strong,
intuitive as well as rational, submissive as well as controlling.
Sexual identity falls away in the transfiguration of sainthood.

Notes

1. Carolyn Heilbrun, *Toward a Recognition of Androgyny*
(New York: Harper and Row, 1973).

2. Heilbrun, *Androgyny*, xiv.

3. Heilbrun, *Androgyny*, xii–xiv.

4. John Henry Newman, *Callista: A Sketch of the Third
Century* (London: Burns and Oates, n.d.).

5. Ian Ker, *John Henry Newman. A Biography* (Oxford:

Clarendon Press, 1988), 734.

6. Ker, *John Henry Newman. A Biography*, 190.

7. Ker, *John Henry Newman. A Biography*, 210.

8. John Henry Newman, *The Idea of a University*, ed. Martin Svaglic (New York: Rinehart and Co., 1960).

9. Heilbrun, *Androgyny*, 118.

10. "The Letter of Paul to the Galatians," *The Holy Bible*, New Revised Standard Version (Nashville: Thomas Nelson, 1989), ch. 3, verses 27–28.

4
Newman and the Intellectual Advancement of Women
Joyce Sugg

Anthony Trollope, a writer beloved of Newman, has a character in one of his novels, an elderly lady of ultra-conservative opinions, who says disapprovingly to a young girl, "They say women are to vote, and become doctors, and if so, there's no knowing what devil's tricks they mightn't do."[1] This novel, *He Knew He Was Right*, written between 1867–68, like most of Trollope's works, is topical both in its incidental references and its social implications. Two women doctors were practicing in England in the eighteen sixties, it was being suggested that women should have the vote and the topic of women's emancipation was in the air. Of course education, the opportunity to enter the professions and political choice must be seen as indivisible. In the decades when Newman was working hard to educate school boys and striving for university education for Catholic young men, good boarding and day schools were being set up by the redoubtable Miss Buss and Miss Beale and by 1890 women were going up to Oxford and Cambridge.

There are no references to these events in Newman's letters and diaries as there are in Trollope's secular novels, nor did he take part in the campaign for the emancipation of women. He did not set about ensuring that women should have more educational opportunities: it would be fair to say that he had enough to do with the tasks he had set himself in the educational field. However, when we read his pleas for a responsible laity it is impossible to lay aside the question of women's role and their education.

He does have a great deal to offer for reflection on the matter of women's intellectual development because of his many friendships with women and his natural and deep sympathy with them. What were they like, these Victorian women who entered into correspondence with Newman? What ideals of Catholic life did they aspire to? What opportunities did they have or lack? And what was Newman's attitude to them?

His general attitudes were shaped of course by his own family life. He was very much a family man, closely linked with his mother and sisters for a long period, when he was an Oriel don, because of affection and his sense of responsibility for them after his father's early death. He got on better with his sisters than with his brothers and they were all intelligent. It was customary for caring and bookish brothers to help their sisters, handing on some of the education they received at school and university to the girls at home: this is a pattern clearly set out in some of the novels of Charlotte Yonge, Keble's protegee. In 1825 Harriett Newman was reading Gibbon and Tasso and John was advising Jemima in mathematics. She was, he said, an ingenious girl who "has invented a very correct illustration of the asymptotic curve."[2] In adult life Harriett published some children's tales in sprightly prose and Jemima became a good amateur pianist.

Women, including those of the Newman family, were concerned with the Oxford Movement, in reading and discussions, in learning its tenets and experiencing its influence on their own religious devotion: Mary, the youngest sister, learned Keble's poems from *The Christian Year*, using her brother's copy. When the Tracts were written ladies helped in the distribution, carrying them when they went visiting.

Newman made friends with the wives of his associates, particularly with Elizabeth, the wife of his great friend, John Bowden, and he was a welcome guest in many homes. All this laid a foundation for his later years when visits were rare but when he was in touch with countless families, writing to many married women and pleased to know their children. He admired the wives and mothers he knew and saw in the lives of many of them that close attention to the faithful carrying out of daily duties that he set down as a requisite for genuine Christian commitment.

A number of Newman's friends became nuns and he held that vocation in high regard. He considered, in his Anglican days that one of the results of the Reformation was to limit women's lives by its exclusion of monasticism.

> I know not any more distressing development of the cruel temper of Protestantism than the determined, bitter and scoffing spirit in which it has set itself against institutions which give dignity and independence to the position of women in society. As matters stand, marriage is almost the only shelter which a defenceless portion of the community has against the rude world.[3]

He was to see the situation change: the Anglican church, inspired by the Oxford Movement and by Pusey in particular, set up convents, and Catholic congregations of nuns in the decades after Newman's conversion proliferated. The new female converts, or their daughters, often turned to the religious life. Newman particularly admired the Good Shepherd nuns, he had links with the Visitation nuns, and he corresponded with Fanny Taylor who founded a congregation called the Poor Servants of the Mother of God to work for the poor.

It is curious that he did not forge links with some congregation specifically dedicated to the work of education. His favorite convent was that of the Dominican Third Order at Stone in Staffordshire. They kept a girls' school but also did nursing and could not be called a congregation specifically concerned with education. Their remarkable foundress, Mother Margaret Hallahan, herself of limited education (she had begun her adult life as a servant girl) had character and devotion enough to attract some forceful and intelligent recruits, including two converts who were Newman's friends. One wrote a life of Mother Margaret that he greatly admired as a good piece of work which would instruct Catholics and help a general levelling up to the same moral and intellectual state of mind among all Christians. In 1846 he spoke enthusiastically of Cornelia Connelly, the American foundress of the Society of the Holy Child Jesus and recommended the new congregation to his friend, Miss Giberne. Its first object would be "instructing girls, principally of the middle and upper classes and," said Newman, "the person who begins it, is in the truest and best sense an enthusiastic person - of education and great influence in her circle" (*LD*, X1, 209). But, later, Newman held it against Mother Connelly that she had quarrelled with Emily Bowles, his friend and protegee, and what could have been another friendship died in the bud. Emily Bowles, as a young religious in the Society of the Holy Child when new foundations were being made took decisions on herself without reference to the Superior, and left after a prodigious row.

She was an intelligent, forceful woman—her very faults proclaim her capabilities—and she is one of the many single women of that time whose talents were frustrated. There was a surplus of women, and spinsters often had a hard time, particularly if they lacked money. Another friend of Newman's, Mary Holmes, illustrates the point. She was a plain, clever woman (he once described her as "very clever and very good" [*LD*, XV111, 498]) who would have liked a musical career but was constrained to work as a governess. She was incurably restless and it seems likely that she did not settle down because her talents were not fully used.

The activities of women, outside the domestic ones of running a home, were generally of an amateur kind. Many of Newman's women friends painted pictures or made music: these were employments that were allowed since they were an extension of the accomplishments that girls of good family were expected to have. To draw and paint, to play the piano, to write stories were all employments for the home. Like the poor seamstresses of a lower class they could work within the declared boundaries.

Some ladies did publish their novels and stories. One saintly, well-born, intelligent Catholic, Lady Georgiana Fullerton, was a best-selling novelist. Many manuscripts of religious tales were sent to Newman for his comments. His sound advice to one aspirant went thus: "As far as your writing a good work goes I think if you formed your plan without reference to religion and only let religious feeling show itself in that spontaneous way in which religious people can't help showing it, you would write in a higher style of art" (*LD*, X1X, 479).

This might be taken as a signal for later generations of lay people. In Newman's day it was necessary for Catholics to proclaim their piety—they needed to establish their identity—but lay activity would need ultimately to be in the secular sphere. But the ladies of Newman's acquaintance were not concerned to enter such professions as medicine, nor to campaign for the vote

Most of these ladies were converts and many could be called Newman's converts since they were strongly influenced by him or actually received into the Church by him. Of course they venerated Newman as he always remembered Walter Mayers with gratitude as the human means by which he came to faith in Christ. The ladies' veneration was, however, somewhat excessive: they wanted to spoil him, flatter, put him on a pedestal. Newman would not be lionized. Hence his disarming letter to Miss Munro in 1850 when he assured her that he had nothing of the saint about him: "It is enough for me to black the saints' shoes - if St Philip uses blacking in heaven."[4] In his Anglican days he had assured Mary Holmes "I am *not* venerable and nothing can make me so."[5] Yet he did not spend all his energy keeping these admirers at arm's length. Instead, he offered friendship. He gave affection, advice and instruction and relied on them very often for sympathy and understanding. At the end of his early account of his illness in Sicily he had written that he felt the lack of that sympathy which a wife would have and wondered if he would ever have spiritual children who would take that kind of interest in him.

The rhetorical question was later answered in the affirmative. It was usually to Emily Bowles that Newman uttered his "growls" when oppressed by the balks that attended his Catholic life. Such is a lengthy letter of May 1863 about the "invisible chain" that bound him, about the destructive power of Propaganda, the "extreme centralization which now is in use" and the suppression of freedom of opinion. He ends, "I never wrote such a letter to anyone yet, and I shall think twice before I send you the whole of it."[6] Nevertheless the letter was sent. There are other letters to her, in the same vein, complaining of the general attitude to the laity and to the stifling of the Oxford scheme. These letters relieved his mind and give readers now some valuable insights into his thinking. Emily Bowles was not the only recipient of such confidences. A letter to Charlotte Wood in December 1866 is another frank complaint which ends, "I never wrote thus plainly and fully to any person yet" (LD, XX11, 327) and a series of letters to Mrs. Bowden and to Mrs. William Froude, about the time of his conversion to Rome, give his mind very fully. He had a great reliance on his friends' discretion and made other assumptions when he wrote to them, that they would understand the complexities of his troubles with ecclesiastical authority, would be interested in arguments for less centralization in the Church, university education for Catholic youths and so on. He did not try to present a bland picture of a church that was faultless, nor did he simplify or smooth matters because he was talking to women.

Newman's letters were much taken up, since he was advising converts, with discussion of theological difficulties, of advice and recommendations for further reading. He said once to Emily Bowles, having compared the writing of theology to "dancing on the tight rope some hundred feet above the ground" that, "Ladies can't be in the position to try" (LD, XXII, 215). All the same, every Christian, in his or her degree, must engage the mind in theological reflection. Many of the women that Newman instructed were intelligent, well-read and articulate. Newman followed his own rule, to treat each individual according to need and capacity, and he certainly did not treat women as fools.

One very exacting convert, intellectually, was a Mrs. Helbert who asked a good many searching questions. Newman said to her, "you must recollect you have chosen a man's part, you have chosen to go by antiquity, by the Fathers, by history, and to ask answers to questions arising thence" (*LD*, XXIV, 274). It is typical of the times that there is the assumption that such a stance belongs to a man but it is typical of Newman that he accepted her intellectual bent and answered accordingly. Other intelligent questioning women, Lady Georgina Chatterton, Mrs. William Froude amongst others, received sympathetic teaching suited to their minds.

We know from Newman's comments on the enforced idleness of Catholic youths kept from the universities and on the sad plight of convert Anglican clergy who were out of work that he desired people to have a suitable object in life. He encouraged many women in charitable work to ameliorate the sad condition of the poor, so vividly chronicled by novelists of the time, not Trollope but Dickens and Mrs. Gaskell. He also tried to band them together for prayer and mutual support in their charitable endeavors: he wanted to enrol women in the Little Oratory, an organization for men, and we find him, according to his diary, saying Mass on 9 August 1857 for the Pia Unio, this being a federation of women responsible, amongst other things, for the guild of young women in the Oratory parish.

He also entrusted tasks to his women friends, individually, though it was late in his life that he found a specifically intellectual work for a woman to do. This was when he entrusted the putting together of selected letters of his Anglican years to Anne Mozley, his relative by Jemima's marriage. She proved to be a careful, judicious editor and carried out the work to Newman's satisfaction.

One of the most interesting episodes in the history of the Oratory School was the quarrel Newman had with the first headmaster, Nicholas Darnell and the part played by Frances Wootten in the affair. She was an old friend and a convert, put in charge of the domestic arrangements and having particular charge of young and delicate boys. Newman had great faith in her and the other "Dames," be-lieving that they made the school more of a home and that they helped to instil Christian principles. They were, in their way, as important as schoolmasters. Newman had a great regard for Mrs. Wootten's opinions, saying, for instance, when giving his views on the fostering of priestly vocations that he had consulted her "and found her of the same mind" (*LD*, XX, 22), as though that clinched the matter.

When Nicholas Darnell, who wished to distance the school from Newman and the Oratory, delivered his ultimatum that either he would go or Mrs. Wootten must go, Newman gave decisively in her favor. His reasons were couched in chivalrous terms but there was more to the affair than this. Newman was not striking out for the intellectual advancement of women—Frances Wootten had no desire to be teaching Greek rather than supervising kitchen and sick-rooms—but he was underlining his view that education is for the whole person. Darnell would give priority to academic achievement in the classroom, the boys to be spurred on by beatings, and he thought less of religious instruction and the gentle fostering of the Dames. Newman disagreed. His respect for women is well illustrated here.

Right at the end of his life Newman wrote a significant letter to his niece, Jane Mozley. She had acquired a position in life as housekeeper to her brother who was a schoolmaster who took pupils in as boarders. This was no great advancement but it gave her "an object in life" (the favorite phrase again). He went on:

> I congratulate you on having got one. I trust and pray it may be a success. It is one of the best points of this unhappy age, that it has made so many openings for the activity of women. (*LD*, XXX, 316)

So far, so good. However, the expectations and opportunities of his niece, of Emily Bowles, Mary Holmes and the rest of them were still exceedingly narrow. If the Church was to have what Newman so earnestly desired, an active and educated laity, the women would need to have those advantages that he so graphically described when pleading for a university education for Catholic young men. He spoke of Catholics having been thrust aside and deprived of the education which would enable them to manage land and money and to govern the country, and went on:

> The time is come when this moral disability must be removed. Our desideratum is, not the manners and habits of gentlemen; - these can be, and are, acquired in other ways, by good society, by foreign travel, by the innate grace and dignity of the Catholic mind; - but the force, the steadiness, the comprehensiveness and the versatility of intellect the command over our own powers, the instinctive, just estimate of things as they pass before us, which sometimes indeed is a natural gift, but commonly is not gained without much effort and the exercise of years.[7]

The women Newman had as friends were gentlewomen (in the best sense) and they were thinking people, far more intellectually deprived and lacking in responsible employments than the Catholic youths who suffered these disabilities. Few, at the time of Newman's utterance, would think to transpose the passage to describe the plight of women and he certainly would not have done so for he was in many ways innately conservative. But his emphasis on the value of education, his insistence that the laity should form their minds and work responsibly in the Church and for the general good, and his trust in women's capabilities, add up to make an implicit program for emancipation. The conservative old lady, in Trollope's novel, would have found Newman dangerous.

Notes

1. Anthony Trollope, *He Knew He Was Right* (London: World's Classics edition, Oxford University Press, 1985), 111.

2. Meriol Trevor, *The Pillar of the Cloud* (London: Macmillan, 1962), 56.

3. John Henry Newman, *Letters on the Church of the Fathers*, cited by Ian Ker, *John Henry Newman. A Biography* (Oxford: Clarendon Press, 1990), 190.

4. Joyce Sugg, *A Packet of Letters* (London: Oxford University Press, 1983), 84.

5. Sugg, *A Packet of Letters*, 58.

6. Sugg, *A Packet of Letters*, 137–40.

7. John Henry Newman, *The Idea of a University* (1873), edited with introduction and notes by I. T. Ker (Oxford: Clarendon Press, 1976); the passage is taken from the Preface.

5
Newman's Crisis-Trope in the *Apologia*
Eugene Hollahan

George Eliot singled out the strange New Testament word
crisis as a master trope and arguably the most characterizing
single word in the modern world. Eliot's "charter" (so to speak)
for any subsequent study of her "great noun"—to be found in
Chapter XI of *Felix Holt, the Radical* (1866)—places a burden
squarely upon those who would investigate the varieties of
human discourse that have shaped modern consciousness.
Beginning with the invention of the novel, the extraordinary
career of the *crisis*-trope constitutes an essential element in
modern sensibility. By means of its tropical twistings and
turnings under the hands of major authors composing their
masterpieces—within cultural contexts including theology, philosophy, social science, psychology, and the like—the great noun
forcefully proves its special potency.

Eliot's great trope comes into full efflorescence in the
conflicted twentieth century. Throughout western culture, it signifies modern anxiety and responses to anxiety. *Crisis* also becomes increasingly functional in numerous jargons, as a
buzzword intended to trigger unthinking responses.

The crisis-anxiety of the twentieth century has produced
utterances in all areas of culture, including major statements by
a theologian (Karl Barth), a philosopher (Edmund Husserl), a
historian of science (T. S. Kuhn), and a social scientist (Jürgen
Habermas). Their utterances might constitute materials for a separate study of *crisis*-rhetoric, but here they serve to contextualize
the study of serious novels.

Critical attention to such extreme *crisis*-rhetorics as Barth's can be justified in the same way that the French ethnographer Marcel Mauss justifies his close study of certain primitive societies: "the maximum, the excessive, which make it possible to see better the facts than where, not less essential, they remain small and involuted."[1] In his influential "theology of KRISIS," Barth puts his own distinctive stamp upon the great noun. He pushes the trope well beyond its narrowly standard limits, displaying it as a pure verbal force and a crucial invention of the human spirit. He compels *crisis* to serve not merely as a noun of substance or condition but to some degree as a noun of corporeality, a trope that bodies forth man's struggle for existence. Thus he witnesses to an agonized modern subjectivity transforming itself within an increasingly rationalistic, manipulative culture.

Tracing the diachronic development of a figure of speech through several centuries offers abundant pleasure as the journey twists through major literary works and famous authorial names. Steadily throughout the nineteenth century, the great noun *crisis* and its attendant crisis-consciousness became both an individual and a corporate means for dealing with reality. It became increasingly a method for making statements, authorizing opinions, describing and characterizing social changes, and engaging in political and ideological struggles. To ignore *crisis* would be to ignore reality and the means of having control over reality. The century was vexed, enlivened, and radically altered by numerous ideologies, visionary theories and systematic programs urging conflicting assumptions and goals. Ideologies that provided context and motivation for new forms of consciousness included (to name but a few) Romanticism, Utilitarianism, Positivism, and Liberalism. They triggered or enabled *crisis*-structured experiences both actual and fictive. Ideologies always demand an assertive Nay or Yea, and ideologies themselves also undergo crisis.[2] Nineteenth-century authors responded to emergent ideologies in crisis by depicting individuals whose existences are shaped or who self-consciously shape their own existences via a *crisis*-trope.

Three major Victorian sages—Thomas Carlyle, John Stuart

Mill, and John Henry Newman—composed famous accounts of their own ordeals precipitated by a powerful Utilitarianism or Liberalism. They contribute to the context for the history of *crisis*-consciousness in the novel. A plausible approach to these three writers is afforded by a *crisis*-utterance from another sage, Matthew Arnold. In the same year as Eliot's *Felix Holt, the Radical*, Arnold wittily enunciated his major theme: the cultural centrality of sound critical thinking. For Arnold, to possess crisis-consciousness amounts to standing "at the centre" of things.

> I have got into much trouble for calling my countrymen Philistines, and all through these remarks I am determined never to use that word; but I wonder if there can be anything offensive in calling one's countryman a young man from the country. I hope not; and if not, I should say, for the benefit of those who have seen Mr. John Parry's amusing enter- tainment, that England and Englishmen, holding forth on *some great crisis in a foreign country*,—Poland, say, or Italy,—are apt to have on foreigners very much the effect of the young man from the country, who talks to the nursemaid after she has upset the perambulator. There is *a terrible crisis*, and the discourse of the young man from the country, excellent in itself, is *felt not to touch the crisis vitally*. Nevertheless, on he goes; the perambulator lies a wreck, the child screams, the nursemaid wrings her hands, the old gentleman storms, the policeman gesticulates, the crowd thickens; still, that astonishing young man talks on, serenely unconscious that *he is not at the centre* of the situation.[3] (emphasis added)

Crisis-imagination has come to represent a *sine qua non* for a truly civilized life. Twentieth-century novelists such as Forster and Robert Coover will self-consciously echo Arnold's linking of *crisis*-experience to some metaphorical center of reality, nation- alistic or metaphysical. More broadly in the nineteenth century, Arnold's type of crisis-consciousness reflected a kind of general preoccupation that would animate many forms of discourse.[4]

In his wildly energetic spiritual autobiography, *Sartor Resartus: The Life and Opinions of Herr Teufelsdröckh*,[5] Carlyle employs *crisis* one single time to signal his hero's anguished tropological turn from negativism (pessimism) to positivism (optimism). *Sartor Resartus* urges several kinds of doctrines —metaphysical, ethical, social—intended to redress an insincerely costumed England. It depicts Germanic philosophical idealism in conflict with a shadowy but forceful Calvinism, a turn against turn which produces in Carlyle a painful impasse. Carlyle's own personal turmoil, by which he earned the right to speak as a sage, finds expression in three central chapters. In a prolonged moment of truth—"The Everlasting No," "The Centre of Indifference," "The Everlasting Yea"—Carlyle develops the equivalence of a plotted crisis and climax. In "The Everlasting Nay," Teufelsdröckh reasons that a vast utilitarian machine grinds joy out of human life. The "nay" uttered here is two-pronged. He sadly acknowledges the widespread modern disbelief in life's supposed purpose, but then he defiantly says "nay" to this negative scheme of things. In "The Centre of Indifference," he wanders between two worlds, a mechanistic realism and a dynamic idealism. In "The Everlasting Yea," he resolutely makes a three-part judgment or choice: to renounce false hopes of happiness, accept human sorrow as a holy condition, and carry out a practical plan for his life. By surviving this chastening turn of events, Teufelsdröckh has earned the right to offer his nugget of truth to his bewildered fellow-men.

Carlyle's fictive editor presents an account of Teufelsdröckh's agonies as a fever-crisis.

> Under the strange nebulous envelopment, wherein our Professor has now shrouded himself, no doubt but his spiritual nature is nevertheless progressive, and growing: for how can the 'Son of Time,' in any case, stand still? We behold him, through those dim years, *in a state of crisis, of transition*: his mad Pilgrimings, and general solution into aimless Discontinuity, what is all this but a mad Fermentation; wherefrom, the fiercer it is, the clearer product will one day evolve itself?[6] (emphasis added)

Carlyle enriches the tradition by offering his reader the chemical metaphor of *crisis* as a purifying process within human consciousness. Thus he depicts a tropological shift from metonymic mechanism to synecdochic vitalism. More precisely, Carlyle's economical crisis-trope informs the first half of *Sartor Resartus* so as to depict a shift from metaphor, through metonymy and synecdoche (the sartorial anatomy of society), to irony; then, in the second half, a new metaphor (vitalism of work) appears as rationale and motive for new consciousness and new behavior.

J. S. Mill chose to express his own personal crisis and the new consciousness it afforded him not by means of symbolic narrative but by analytical exposition within an autobiography. As important as *Sartor Resartus*, Mill's *Autobiography*[7] was written over a long period of time, partly before 1861, partly after 1871. An economist, logician, and moral philosopher, he labored to defend *laissez faire* capitalism even while being acutely aware of its potential abuses. He supported liberal political and social innovations. The *Autobiography* consists of seven chapters, the titles of which clearly display Mill's use of the great noun to structure his anguished, inspiring story.

Mill's famous fifth chapter depicts experiences important to his own personal development and to the intellectual history of nineteenth-century England. It illustrates Brown's dialectical premise (adapted from T. S. Kuhn) that crisis enables progress. A summary of Chapter V reveals how Mill, in 1826–27, experienced the personal agony that led him to swing back from subjection to his father's strict Benthamite dogma and regimen.

Mill began his adult life intending to become a "reformer of the world," but at age twenty he fell into an inexplicable depression. His account of this anguish somewhat resembles Carlyle's experience of a rejection by the universe, as it were the negative side of Carlyle's Everlasting No. Like George Eliot, Mill establishes a strong link between *crisis* and *consciousness*.

> In this frame of mind it occurred to me to put the question directly to myself: "Suppose that all your objects in life were realized; that all the changes in institutions and opinions which you are looking forward to, could be completely effected at this very instant: would this be a great joy and happiness to you?" And *an irrepressible self-consciousness distinctly answered, "No!"* At this my heart sank within me: the whole foundation on which my life was constructed fell down. All my happiness was to have been found in the continual pursuit of this end. The end had ceased to charm, and how could there ever again be any interest in the means? I seemed to have nothing left to live for.[8]

Mill judged that the habit of logical analysis had worn away his emotional life, so he decided upon suicide if his problem were not solved within one year. Happily, he found a way out of his despair, beginning with the moment when he was "moved to tears" by reading Marmontel's *Memoires*. He began to make the stressful transition from one system to another. Much like Carlyle, he experiences up to the moment of his crisis a shift from metaphor (filial piety) through metonymy and synecdoche (Utilitarian principles and classifications) to irony (self-loathing); then, happily, he reconstitutes a new metaphoric basis for life (affectivity). As candidly as possible, Mill describes his own personal crisis as a turning point in terms of happiness properly valued as a desirable end rather than a means to social improvement. He announces: "This theory now became the basis of my philosophy of life." Premises underlying his tropological shift from an analytical to an affective schema represented for

Mill himself "turning points, marking a definite progress in my mode of thought."

Newman likewise structured his own spiritual autobiography—*Apologia Pro Vita Sua*[9]—by using Eliot's great noun one single time. Both Carlyle's *crisis*-transition from self-conscious individualism to an un-self-conscious work ethic and Mill's *crisis*-transition from his father's closed system to a more open philosophy are matched in narrative excitement and cultural significance by what Newman—perhaps echoing Paine—called his "great revolution." While pursuing absolute truth as well as defying a dominant Liberalism, Newman changed his allegiance from Protestantism (metaphor) to Roman Catholicism (synecdoche). Given the suave clarity and clear logic of Newman's thought-style, his argument can be easily summarized. Newman, of course, had spearheaded the Tractarian or Oxford Movement which sought to restore the Anglican Church to its former truth and glory. Chapter I recounts how he modified his narrow-minded Protestant dislike of the Roman Catholic Church. Chapter II narrates his participation in the Oxford Movement, which aspired to return England from pathlessness to the right path. Gradually, he realized that he could in fact accede to some few Roman Catholic dogmas. In 1841, Newman published Tract XC, where he in effect asked himself: "Can I be saved in the English Church?" Compelled to answer in the negative, he decided to enter the Roman Catholic Church and be ordained a priest. In Chapter V, he argues that for an individual to be tested in a conflict between authority and private judgment can be salutary to one's moral fiber. Newman's "great revolution of mind" is free of Carlyle's and Mill's romantic self-glorification. Whereas their books are explicitly structured by a single *crisis*-trope precisely enabling a moment of change in a main plot, Newman himself does also use the great noun one single time but judiciously places it so as to achieve an entirely different, non-egotistical emphasis. The general effect is to convey a quality of modesty unlike the egotism of Carlyle and Mill and much more consistent with the sweet temper normally associated with Newman.

The effect of the *Apologia* was not like a recollection of some long-past event but rather "like a conversational explosion" on the subject of a recent event.[10] His single explicit designation of an event as a concussive *crisis* occurs not at the turning point of his own personal adventure but at the beginning of a collective adventure, the Oxford Movement itself. In Chapter II, in a context of pious admiration for the men who influenced him in his spiritual development, Newman describes how the Anglo-Catholic party had suddenly become a power in the national church. He designates the early stages of the Oxford Movement as "the birth of a crisis."

> Its originators would have found it difficult to say what they aimed at of a practical kind: rather, they put forth views and principles for their own sake, because they were true, as if they were obliged to say them; and, as they might be themselves surprised at their earnestness in uttering them, they had as great cause to be surprised at the success which attended their propagation. And, in fact, they could only say that those doctrines were in the air; that to assert was to prove, and that to explain was to persuade; and that the Movement in which they were taking part was the *birth of a crisis* rather than of a place. (*Apo.*, 69–70, emphasis added)

As a *crisis*-conscious apologist, Newman subordinates himself to the activities of the group. Ironically, of course, the *Apologia* may in fact depict a personal transformation not only as compelling as that in Carlyle and Mill but equally egotistical. Newman could actually intend thus to de-center both Aristotelian logical structure and the members of the Oxford Movement from any privileged place in his narrative. More likely, though, he expresses an authentic humility.

Carlyle, Mill, and Newman (three sages thrown into crisis by the nay-saying power of dominant ideologies) after uttering an anguished Nay conclude by uttering a hard-earned Yea. These three spiritual autobiographies of Victorian Sages bear directly upon my study of narrative *crisis*-tropes. Although themselves not novels, these self-scrutinizing forms of consciousness nevertheless flesh out the history of *crisis*-narratives by contextualizing the novelists who structure their representations via the great trope.

Notes

1. Cited in J. Hillis Miller, *Fiction and Repetition: Seven English Novels* (Cambridge: Harvard University Press, 1982), 4.

2. Tony Bennett, *Formalism and Marxism* (New York: Methuen, 1979), 155.

3. Matthew Arnold, "My Countrymen," *Culture and Anarchy, with Friendship's Garland and Some Literary Essays*, ed. R. H. Super, in *The Complete Prose Works of Matthew Arnold* (Ann Arbor: University of Michigan Press, 1965), 5: 3–31.

4. Hans Kellner, *Language and Historical Representation: Getting the Story Crooked* (Madison: University of Wisconsin Press, 1989) urges the existence of such a governing or Over-Trope: "a trope that shapes and regulates the tropic differences and combats within it" (214). Given the self-reflexive properties of *crisis*, I think that irony (crisis-irony?) should be considered such an over-trope.

5. Thomas Carlyle, *Sartor Resartus: The Life and Opinions of Herr Teufelsdröckh*, ed. Charles Frederick Harrold (New York: Odyssey, 1937).

6. Thomas Carlyle, *Sartor Resartus*, ed. Charles Frederick Harrold.

7. John Stuart Mill, *Autobiography and Literary Essays* (Toronto: University of Toronto Press, 1981).

8. Mill, *Autobiography and Literary Essays*, Ch. 5, 139, emphasis added.

9. John Henry Newman, *Apologia Pro Vita Sua*, ed. David Delaura (New York: Norton, 1968).

10. London *Times* (June 16, 1864), 12.

Part II

Personal Principle

6

Newman's Personal Principle at Its Source
Marie Brinkman, S.C.L.

More than a few Newman scholars have identified the ground
of his thought in what Edward Sillem has called "the personal
principle." On the face of it, the phrase speaks little more than
Newman's profound perception of a fundamental truth, that
relationship is the source of motivation and growth, of learning
and faith. More critically, the personal principle is, I think, the
inevitable outcome of a deeper force that governed Newman's
spirit from the beginning of his remembered mental life.
Newman lived by the spiritual and intellectual experience of
realization, which became for him a fundamental and variously
articulated principle of mind that has fruitful implications for
uncovering a common source of knowledge and faith.

Newman made it a principle, of course, in his much analyzed
distinction, in the *Grammar of Assent*,[1] between notional and real
assent in faith. But I believe the roots of the principle lie
unexposed in other texts where Newman images, narrates,
dramatizes, and analogizes the action of the mind com-
prehending, reasoning, and believing. In certain of these texts,
it is not the mind's action that he describes, but the effects and
results of its realization. Those effects are the measure of the
principle's power. Realization, as a productive principle, effects
deep change in a person's development—transformations of
mind, of spirit, of relationship itself. It becomes, for example,
the very fecundity of Reason that Newman images so effectively
in the sixth Discourse of *The Idea of a University*, "Knowledge
in Relation to Learning," and issues in the *master-principle* of

knowledge achieved in the habit of judgment, whose description is the centerpiece of the seventh Discourse. The teacher who meets realization in a learner comes to know what Newman perceived in his students, described, and persistently tried to evoke in his hearers: realization of the truth he was seized by himself.

Newman knew the experience from his youth. Two realizations in his adolescent years permanently marked him. The first was "the inward conversion" at fifteen that convinced him of his election to eternal life and made him "rest in the thought of two luminously self-evident beings," God and himself (*Apo.*, 16).[2] The second realization stripped the first of its tendency toward the notion of predestination and, at the same time, profoundly affected his spiritual development. That was his insight into the truth of Thomas Scott's faith in the Trinity, and his holiness of life. Newman's mentor before the evangelical conversion, Walter Mayers, was, in his words, "the human means of this beginning of divine faith in me," whereas Thomas Scott "made a deeper impression on my mind than any other, and [is he] to whom (humanly speaking) I almost owe my soul" (*Apo.*, 16–17).

In each instance, Newman speaks of the books that accompanied the influence of these men: those of an evangelical stamp that Mayers gave him, and those of Scott, including his spiritual autobiography. It will be books that "plant seeds" in Newman's mind, "stain" his imagination, set up conflicts between ideas that end in the "decay and extinction" of what is false. The word can produce in him as profound and personal an effect as can the man; rather, the person and the word become one in influence and power to change. Edward Hawkins and Sumner's *Treatise on Apostolical Preaching* brought Newman to belief in Tradition; Bishop Butler and his *Analogy of Religion* drew him still closer to orthodox Anglicanism. The Fathers of the Church and John Keble became for Newman the human sources of his gradual conversion to the Holy and Apostolic Church of Jesus Christ. The two truths that Keble brought home to him—originally learned, he says, from Butler—were "the doctrine that material phenomena are both the types and the instruments of real things unseen," or, as Newman calls it, the Sacramental system; and the doctrine of probability as sufficient for the assent of faith.

By Newman's own admission Keble transcended Butler's logical exposition of such probability. He cites Keble's ascribing ultimate religious assent, not to probabilities, "but to the living power of faith and love." Unlike probabilities, these have a living Object: "In the vision of that Object they live." Thus it is that the "argument from Probability" becomes an "argument from Personality" (*Apo.*, 28–29). Perceiving this, Newman finds in Keble confirmation of the deepest spiritual and intellectual inclinations he had known since childhood: Truth is known only in relationship. The "personal principle" itself depends for its efficacy on such realization.

Likewise, the principle of Economy, learned initially from Butler's logical and moral analogies, becomes in the writings of Athanasius, Origen, Clement, and Ignatius the bedrock of Newman's analogical imagination. Made personal and dynamic in Keble's sacramental universe, the analogies that Newman had already sensed between the visible and invisible worlds are now charged with all the implications that he points to in his University Sermons. Without tracing the evolution of thought from those sermons to the *Grammar of Assent*, we find the full statement of the principle of realization in that text, written some five or six years after publication of the *Apologia*.

Four concepts come at the meaning, in Newman's own terms, of realization of knowledge and of belief. The first, *real apprehension*, describes a condition of the second, *real assent*; the term *certitude* identifies the fruit of such assent, and the *illative sense* names that which distinguishes real assent as altogether individual, even while given within a common tradition. Newman defines real apprehension as, first, "an experience or information about the concrete" that remains in the memory as an impression. This remembered impression constitutes "the continued presence in our minds as a likeness" of the actual presence that left it there. Innumerable isolate or associated images of real apprehensions become, as it were, the raw material of real assents. Newman writes, "An act of assent . . . is the most perfect and highest of its kind, when it is exercised on propositions, which are apprehended as experiences and images, that is, which stand for things" (*GA*, 38–52, passim).

He exemplifies such an assent by means of an analogy between our initial knowledge of the universe and our experience of conscience. From the succession of perceptions of praise and blame in a parent's demeanor, a child knows of a being external to self who inspires confidence and shame. Conscience, Newman reasons, is not a rule, but a sanction of right conduct, from its twofold quality as "a judgment of the reason and a magisterial dictate." Its effect in us is that of not only a moral sense, but also a sense of duty to another, to whom we are accountable.

In these interrelated acts of the mind, real apprehension and real assent, we see the essence of realization: the perception of a living other, known to be in relation to oneself and before whom one knows oneself. Realization brings with it certain other infallible effects, that signal its quality and its object. Consciousness of the object of conscience, the Other whom one is faithful to, brings a "serenity of mind, . . . a deep peace, a sense of security, . . . and a hope" felt only before an intelligent being, an Other who knows one from within. Further, in complex assent to any truth, he says, there is "a special relaxation and repose of mind, which is the token of certitude," that cannot accompany simple or unreflective assent, conclusion from inferences, investigation, or doubt. He parallels the fruits of certitude in virtue and knowledge: "As the performance of what is right is distinguished by . . . religious peace, so the attainment of what is true is attested by this intellectual security" (*GA*, 101, 168–69).

The source of this kinship in the effects of a right conscience and a right knowing is, I think, the Illative Sense. Unique to each individual, it is "the ratiocinative mind itself," the living mind that enables us to use principles correctly. "It is a rule to itself, and appeals to no judgment beyond its own." It is "a personal gift or acquisition" which, in reasoning, takes its premises and first elements from "personal characteristics." Here is the origin of the principle of realization, one with the nature of the mind itself, working at its best. Both in real assent and in this adumbrated process of inference, the living mind is intimate to itself and to no other. It is no mechanism, no worker of rules, no generalizer from circumstances. But it is, in its perfected power of judgment, "sufficient for the occasion, deciding what ought to be done here and now, by this given person, under these given circumstances." Nothing of mental life could be more personal, more capable of individual realization except the direct gift of light, or the living response of Conscience. But analogy carries Newman even there: "As the structure of the universe speaks to us of Him Who made it, so the laws of the mind are the expression, not of mere constituted order, but of His will. . . . They throw a reflex light on themselves" (*GA*, 275–78). Whatever our inquiry, its methods and materials, our progress in it are under God's oversight.

In this we glimpse the radically personal quality of Newman's mind at work. His intellectual realizations were of a piece with his presence to God. Nothing passed in his mind that was not open to his Creator. The words with which he concludes the *Grammar* were foreseeable:

> Christianity is addressed . . . to minds which are in the normal condition of human nature. . . . Such minds it addresses both through the intellect and through the imagination; creating a certitude of its truth by arguments too various for direct enumeration, too personal and deep for words. . . . It speaks to us one by one, and it is received by us one by one, as the counterpart, so to say, of ourselves, and is real as we are real. (*GA*, 379)

This is a veritable echo of Newman's allusion, in his Discourses on Liberal Knowledge, to the University as "an *alma mater*, knowing her children one by one" (*Idea*, 165).[3]

In that text, Newman brings to a climax his eloquent

exposition of liberal knowledge in a section on judgment, "that master-principle of business, literature, and talent, which gives [one] strength in any subject he chooses to grapple with and enables him to *seize the strong point in it.*" Here, I believe, he speaks of that habit of a matured Reason that he will elaborate on in the *Grammar* as the Illative Sense. The reference to a *principle*, on the one hand, of business and literature, and on the other, of talent, suggests that the habit is exercised with proficiency within a given discipline or field, and by means of an individual's peculiar power of mind and personality. One with the Illative Sense, this habit of judgment is specific to the individual. Again, explaining "enlargement," a key metaphor of Newman's for the nature of liberal learning, he calls it "the mind's energetic and simultaneous action" upon and among new ideas. It is the action of "a formative power, reducing to order and meaning the matter of our acquirements; it is a making the objects of our knowledge subjectively our own." He calls it a locomotion, a movement onward of a "mental centre" to which all that we know and all that we are learning gravitates (*Idea*, 189, 156). The intimate interrelated living knowledge that this enlargement represents is a character, is an identity, an inner life more personal and significant than one's name.

That this does not overstate the nature and quality of the realized knowledge Newman describes is evident in a central passage of the fifth Discourse, where he speaks of it as "impregnated by Reason," the principle of the fecundity of knowledge which makes it sufficient unto itself. Such knowledge, he says, is "an acquired illumination, . . . a habit, a personal possession, and an inward endowment, . . . individual and permanent" (*Idea*, 137–38).

All such words, statements, and elaborations are manifestations of what we mean by realization. That it refers equally to acts of conscience, acts of learning and knowing, acts of judging, and acts of faith does not diminish its clarity for us. Each reference reinforces and makes more vivid the concept of realization as the source and foundation of Newman's "personal principle." These concepts and passages from three unrelated texts written over a span of eighteen years are unified by the steady persistent light of Newman's intelligence, itself fully realized and directed to the end of bringing us to perceive the texture, motion, and potential of our own minds.

That is how he must have appealed to the students of Oxford and later of the Catholic University of Dublin. In his Report for the Year 1854–55 to the Archbishops of Ireland, Newman spoke of the purpose of an *Alma Mater*, "who inspires affection while she whispers truth; who enlists imagination, taste, and ambition on the side of duty." To assist the formal discipline of a university that such a high calling requires, he insisted on the exertion of personal influence, without which the integrity of a place of learning was, he thought, incomplete. Newman went to great lengths to describe the "small communities" in which all students of the University were to live.

"Personal influence," he wrote, "requires personal acquaintance, and the minute labour of a discretionary rule is too fatiguing to be exercised on a large number." In such small learning communities what Newman called the *genius loci, the spirit of a place,* was "the instructor most readily admitted and most affectionately remembered" (*Campaign*, 37, 39).[4] Newman describes in his reports three chief means to this end of community. The first was the establishment of exhibitions at end of term, with public recognition and lucrative prizes. He hoped by this particular tradition to inspire "the respect due to successful talent" and to make those so honored "the centre of influence" among their fellows. More important, of course, were the tutors—an office Newman and Hurrell Froude had held with such success at Oriel College. These were young men no more than two or three years older than their pupils, who had gained honors on examination in their final course of study, and who were "half companions, half advisers" of the students. While preparing these for lectures and examinations, the tutors gained the confidence of the younger men, joined in their recreations, exercised an unparalleled influence, and came to "know more about them than anyone else" (*Campaign*, 40–42).

From professors, too, Newman hoped for a great deal.

Leaving them to their own discretion, he nevertheless trusted that "without effort, and almost spontaneously," they would draw to themselves young men "open to their influence" from a love of learning or from admiration and response to their personal interest.   As Rector, Newman required what he called a catechetical form of instruction and small classes for discussion, either with the professor or with a tutor, of the matter of the weekly lecture.   Without this catechesis and exchange, he insisted, learning was bound to be superficial (*Campaign*, 42, 84).[5] It was the intellectual character Newman was concerned to form in his students. From it would issue integrity, consistency, clarity of thought; from such integrity, illuminated at its Source and enabled by grace, would come moral integrity and truth of the spirit. Nothing was isolate in Newman; nothing separate, unrelated. As truth is one, so is the human spirit in possession of truth; as truth reveals itself in its aspects, so the mind grasps them and makes of all aspects a whole. This is the realization that deepened Newman's understanding, caused his words to catch fire as if struck on flint. They spoke to the realizing spirit of his hearers, his students.

The depth of his convictions about the power of influence in a community of learners had its roots in his own experience in that role; for the sake of their common belief in what a tutor should be, Newman and Froude had lost their tutorial jobs. Now, writing to the Bishops, Newman said:

> In this idea of a College Tutor, we see that union of intellectual and moral influence, the separation of which is the evil of the age. Men are accustomed to go to the Church for religious training, but to the world for the cultivation both of their hard reason and their susceptible imagination.   A Catholic University will but half remedy this evil, if it aims only at professional, not at private teaching. Where is the private teaching, there will be the real influence. (*Campaign*, 120)

Given Newman's repeated emphases, "private teaching"

means the personal influence of mind-upon-mind among peers, between pupil and tutor, between professor and student. In the following year, writing of the history of the Universities, he speaks of this living bond:

> The academic celebrations of a University issue in the promotion of a certain living and, as it were, bodily communication of knowledge from one to another. . . . of an enlargement of mind, intellectual and social, of an ardent love of the particular study, which may be chosen by each individual, and a noble devotion to its interests. (*HS*, III, 13)[6]

And again, he calls on the nature of religious teaching to clarify the immediacy of the effects of secular knowledge: The former "concurs in the principle of a University so far as this, that its great instrument, or rather organ, has ever been that which nature prescribes in all education, the personal presence of a teacher, or . . . Oral Tradition." Newman then images the encounter with truth, toward which all teaching tends:

> It is the living voice, the breathing form, the expressive countenance, which preaches, which catechises. Truth, a subtle, invisible, manifold spirit, is poured into the mind of the scholar by his eyes and ears, through his affection, imagination, and reason; it is poured into his mind and is sealed up there in perpetuity. (*HS*, III, 14–15)

In his essay, "The Tamworth Reading Room, By Catholicus," Newman chides Sir Robert Peel for countenancing, in his support of the Library at Tamworth, the school of thought which held that excellence could come "not from within, but from without," from a "passive exposure to influences over which we have no control." Newman gives us, then, the most memorable expression of the "personal principle":

> The heart is commonly reached, not through the reason, but through the imagination, by means of direct impression, by the testimony of facts and events, by history, by description.

> Persons influence us, voices melt us, looks subdue us, deeds
> inflame us. . . . No one, I say, will die for his own
> calculations; he dies for realities. (*DA*, 266–93)[7]

Realization of reality was the peculiar work of the mind, as
Newman perceived it. He criticized Döllinger—Church historian,
who rejected the declaration of Papal infallibility in Vatican I
with an appeal to history—for the quality of his thinking:

> He is not . . . a philosophical historian. . . . He does not *throw
> himself* into the *state of things* which he reads about, he does
> not *enter into* the *position* of Honorius, or of the Council 40
> years afterwards. He ties you down like Shylock to the letter
> of the bond, instead of *realizing what took place as a scene.*[8]
> (Newman's emphasis)

Here again we see by contrast Newman's experience of his
own mind. From its realizations he taught. In the supplementary
lectures which, with the Discourses, make up *The Idea of a
University*, Newman wrote of the University preacher in words
we know he would apply as well to the teacher:

> It is this direct bearing of the teacher on the taught, of his
> mind upon their minds, and the mutual sympathy which exists
> between them, which is his strength and influence when he
> addresses them. They hang upon his lips as they cannot hang
> upon the pages of his book. . . Thought and word . . . must
> issue fresh and fresh, as from the preacher's mouth, so from
> his breast, if they are to be "spirit and life" to the hearts of his
> hearers. (*Idea*, 388)

We come now full circle from the adolescent realization of
"God and myself"—that Newman recorded as the first real
apprehension of realities to which he gave full assent with
certitude—to a conviction of equal force, some forty years later.
From that early experience of a real relationship between himself
and God Newman evolved the first principle of all he wrote and
taught about learning and belief. Edward Sillem summarizes it

admirably: "The growth and development of our knowledge depends on the living dynamism, the alertness and activities of our minds, and above all on our maintaining cognitive relations with the particular things presented to us in experience" (*Phil.N.*, I, 97).[9]

Such knowledge inspires that outrageous claim at the opening of Section 2 of the eighth Discourse: "Right reason, that is, Reason rightly exercised, leads the mind to the Catholic Faith" (*Idea*, 194). That faith is born of the meeting of an individual intelligence with its Source in the Mind of God, and of some partial realization of a recognition. As the person is one, so is the intelligence, understanding or believing Truth, which is, ultimately, one. The *mental centre*, a celebrated but not fully clarified term of the Discourses, is, I take it, the constant growth and moving forward of this dynamic personal power, transforming all one meets into a quest for and discovery of truth.

This brings us to that aspect of realization which produces a community of learners, a living tradition; more, the heart of an institution. Magnanimity in Newman was of his mind, and required a community of minds. "In the nature of things," he wrote, "greatness and unity go together; excellence implies a centre. And such . . . is a University." For Newman an *alma mater* was the mother of truth, the nurturer of the mind, and the home of learning.

Like the deep need of the spirit to which the preacher brings the Word, so the University, he wrote,

> has ever consisted . . . in wants which it alone can satisfy, . . . in the communication of knowledge and the relation and bond which exists between the teacher and the taught. Its constituting, animating principle is this moral attraction of one class of persons to another; which is prior in its nature, nay commonly in its history, to any other tie whatever. (*HS*, III, 16, 48–49)

As is common with Newman, and implicit in his guiding

principle, a key concept, to be fully comprehended, must be realized. This bond between the teacher and the taught, which he generalizes as an attraction between two classes of persons, is the very hunger of the mind for truth and the desire to impart truth, once possessed, to another.

That the desire can become a passion and the hunger a demand is realized in the life or writing of every real teacher. That the bond could be realized in a living tradition and a place, called University, is a possibility that, after the medievals, only a Newman could conceive, first, for his beloved Oxford, then for the Catholic University of Dublin. Once conceived, the idea became a dream and a vision. Since, it has become a call for the rest of us to follow.

Notes

1. John Henry Newman, *Grammar of Assent*, with an Introduction by Étienne Gilson (Garden City, NY: Doubleday, 1955).

2. John Henry Newman, *Apologia Pro Vita Sua*, ed. David J. DeLaura (New York: W. W. Norton, 1968).

3. John Henry Newman, *The Idea of a University*, Introduction by George N. Shuster (Garden City, NY: Doubleday, 1959).

4. John Henry Newman, *My Campaign in Ireland, Part I.* Catholic University Reports and Other Papers, Printed for Private Circulation Only (Aberdeen: A. King, 1896), Report for the Year 1854–55. Archives, Birmingham Oratory.

5. Postscript to the Report of the Organization of the Catholic University of Dublin (October, 1851).

6. Ch. 1, Introductory (written in 1856), in John Henry Newman, *Historical Sketches* (Westminster, Md.: Christian Classics, 1970).

7. John Henry Newman, *Discussions and Arguments on Various Subjects*, 4th ed. (London: Pickering, 1882).

8. Plummer Letters, 41, April, 22, 1870 – February, 23, 1887

(MS with a Set of Unpublished Letters), 172. Archives, Birmingham Oratory.

9. "Newman's Doctrine of Personal Liberalism," *The Philosophical Notebook of John Henry Newman*, 2 vols., ed. Edward Sillem (Louvain: Nauwelaerts Publishing House, 1969).

Newman and Arnold: Liberalism
Tempered by Reflection
Harvey Kerpneck

The centerpiece of any attempt to understand the influence of John Henry Newman on Matthew Arnold must be Arnold's glowing tribute to Newman in *Culture and Anarchy*. The passage occurs just beyond the mid-point of "Sweetness and Light," which is Chapter I of the book as we now have it, that is, of the book Arnold formed from his Oxford lectures when he gathered them, amended them, and published them together. Although everyone is familiar with the passage, it might be as well to refresh our memory of it, so I will quote it entire. Arnold has just been savaging Mr. Gladstone and "the young lions of the *Daily Telegraph*" for the avidity with which they feed the appetite for self-esteem of the mercantile classes and those in general who believe that the foundation for a better England is "material well-being." Then he goes on:

Oxford, the Oxford of the past, has many faults; and she has heavily paid for them in defeat in isolation, in want of hold upon the modern world. Yet we in Oxford, brought up amidst the beauty and sweetness of that beautiful place, have not failed to seize one truth,—the truth that beauty and sweetness are essential characters of a complete human perfection. When I insist on this, I am all in the faith and tradition of Oxford. I say boldly that this our sentiment for beauty and sweetness, our sentiment against hideousness and rawness, has been at the bottom of our attachment to so many beaten causes, of our opposition to so many triumphant movements. And the sentiment is true, and has never been wholly defeated, and has

shown its power even in its defeat. We have not won our
political battles, we have not carried our main points, we have
not stopped our adversaries' advance, we have not marched
victoriously with the modern world; but we have told silently
upon the mind of the country, we have prepared currents of
feeling which sap our adversaries' position when it seems
gained, we have kept up our own communications with the
future. Look at the course of the great movement which
shook Oxford to its centre some thirty years ago! It was
directed, as any one who reads Dr. Newman's *Apology* may
see, against what in one word may be called "Liberalism."
Liberalism prevailed; it was the appointed force to do the work
of the hour; it was necessary, it was inevitable that it should
prevail. The Oxford movement was broken, it failed; our
wrecks are scattered on every shore:—
     'Quae regio in terris nostri non plena laboris?'
But what was it, this Liberalism, as Dr. Newman saw it, and
as it really broke the Oxford movement? It was the great
middle-class Liberalism, which had for the cardinal points of
its belief the Reform Bill of 1832, and local self-government,
in politics; in the social sphere, free-trade, unrestricted
competition, and the making of large industrial fortunes; in the
religious sphere, the Dissidence of Dissent and the
Protestantism of the Protestant religion. I do not say that other
and more intelligent forces than this were not opposed to the
Oxford movement: but this was the force which really beat it;
this was the force which Dr. Newman felt himself fighting
with; this was the force which till only the other day seemed
to be the paramount force in this country, and to be in possession of the future; this was the force whose achievements
fill Mr. Lowe with such inexpressible admiration, and whose
rule he was so horror-struck to see threatened. And where is
this great force of Philistinism now? It is thrust into the
second rank, it is become a power of yesterday, it has lost the
future. A new power has suddenly appeared, a power which
it is impossible yet to judge fully, but which is certainly a
wholly different force from middle-class Liberalism; different
in its cardinal points of belief, different in its tendencies in
every sphere. It loves and admires neither the legislation of
middle-class vestries, nor the unrestricted competition of

middle-class industrialists, nor the dissidence of middle-class Dissent and the Protestantism of middle-class Protestant religion. I am not now praising this new force, or saying that its own ideals are better; all I say is, that they are wholly different. And who will estimate how much the currents of feeling created by Dr. Newman's movement, the keen desire for beauty and sweetness which it nourished, the deep aversion it manifested to the hardness and vulgarity of middle-class Liberalism, the strong light it tuned on the hideous and grotesque illusions of middle-class Protestantism,—who will estimate how much all these contributed to swell the tide of secret dissatisfaction which has mined the ground under the self-confident liberalism of the last thirty years, and has prepared the way for its sudden collapse and supersession? It is in this manner that the sentiment of Oxford for beauty and sweetness conquers, and in this manner long may it continue to conquer![1]

This is vintage Arnold and it would be idle to argue that the passage is *simply* a tribute to Newman. Arnold is here using Newman as he elsewhere uses Wordsworth, Heine, Senancourt, Sophocles, even Homer, as he sets up his culture-heroes who form "touchstones" for his readers to use to investigate "where they are and what they ought to be," as he puts it in the little poem *Self-Dependence*. But it is a glorious tribute nevertheless and one that is strikingly bold, since in the passage Arnold is reminding his Oxford listeners what form their traditions have recently taken and what obligations that recent history confers on them. Or, in other words, Arnold pays Newman this extraordinary tribute in the place many Protestants still believe, as Arnold speaks, to have been defiled by Newman's presence and betrayed by his movement to the Church of Rome and at the very time that the No-Popery sentiments, to which he refers so scathingly in the next chapter, "Doing as One Likes," and the Murphy riots were in full swing. Arnold's injunction to Oxford to be true to itself, to follow Newman in his endeavor to undermine the hardness and vulgarity of middle-class liberalism and the hideous and grotesque illusions of middle-class

Protestantism, is issued to an Oxford still shaking its head over Newman and surrounded by a country gripped by anti-Catholic rioting and hostility and still, at one level, not at all reconciled to the legalization of the Catholic Church in England.

In this context, it was a mark of Arnold's real esteem for Newman, and not simply another manifestation of his perennial desire to *epater les bourgeois*, that he paid him this tribute. In the passage Newman and poetry are conflated and the Oxford Movement, to which English Protestantism is by no means as yet reconciled, is held up as a standard by which Oxford—that is, the enlightened and the concerned and those with the power to translate their enlightenment and concern into action—are to govern themselves.

I started with this passage because while it is easy to stress the obvious differences between the doctrines Arnold and Newman subscribe to, it is even easier to overlook the depth and the passion and the affection in Arnold's uses of and references to Newman in his writings. And this is the more fatal of the errors that are liable to distort the results when one is considering the effects of Newman upon Arnold. Arnold himself was in no doubt about Newman's influences upon him. On October 16, 1869, Arnold wrote to his mother: "When George Sand and Newman go, there will be no writers left living from whom I have received a strong influence." But even if we lacked such a statement, the evidences are so numerous that it seems difficult to believe that anyone broadly familiar with the writings of both men should doubt not only the intricacy of the connection but the authenticity of the link—that is, should doubt that Arnold was deeply indebted to Newman and that, appearances of difference notwithstanding, Matthew Arnold would have been a different thinker, writer, rhetorician had Newman not preceded him and shown him the way—if I could adapt an image in which Arnold praises his father, Dr. Thomas Arnold, in *Rugby Chapel* and apply it to Dr. Arnold's *bete noire*, Newman.

While the likeness seems most pronounced in the tone and style of the two men, there are, besides the *differences* in doctrine, essential points of similarity. Arguing influence is always hard and likeness need not signify much. But many of the likenesses in Arnold to Newman's ideas or to his presentations of his points of view are part of a vast web of intertextured references in which at one time Newman himself is mentioned, at another time the name occurs together with his ideas, at another time his style, and at times simply his ideas. But it is necessary to insist that a very large number of the references to Newman's doctrines or ideas that are found in Arnold are accompanied by mention of Newman by name. Those references that simply allude to or invoke a doctrine are much less numerous than the other kinds.

But part of the problem in estimating the nature of the influence of the older on the younger man clearly arises from external causes. I deliberately invoked the hostility between Dr. Thomas Arnold, the great headmaster of Rugby, and Newman. It is easy to assume that, even if Arnold did not share his father's detestation of Newman, and even if his relationship to his father was as complicated as that relationship tends to be when it is between a magistral father and a brilliant son, Arnold inherited enough of his father's disrelish for Newman that while Newman could be an influence on Arnold, he was not an integral influence but rather one from which we could easily separate the "true" Arnold and see him steadily and see him whole. Another part of the problem arises—at least for some of us—from the differences between *our* political arrangements and those of England in the nineteenth century.   At the centre of the Newman-Arnold relationship is the relationship between Liberalism (sometimes small-l but sometimes upper-case) and Conservatism. We in Canada, being approximately a century closer to British political arrangements than those in the United States, have an advantage in this. Except in my own province, Ontario, where a democratic socialist government has recently been elected to power, and with a large majority, politics in Canada tends to be a constant oscillation between Liberal and Conservative; the parties constantly succeed one another in power. But from what I know of American political arrangements, your only Liberal party is found in New York state—or was, the last time I was aware of it—and in federal politics you have no need of a Conservative party, being amply endowed with the Republican one. This poses a formidable obstacle to understanding the uses of the terms in Victorian Britain and requires an act of historical imagination, thrusting out of sight the modern American equivalents, to get at the Victorian analogues. Even the flexibility of the terms, as their use developed in Victorian society, presents a problem (remember that Anthony Trollope applied *both* terms to himself, calling himself a *Conservative-Liberal*), since as your last election demonstrated, at least one of the terms, *liberal*, tends to be thought of not denotatively but as a tar-brush with which to darken the image of opponents. And to the extent that to understand Newman's influence on Arnold entails understanding the differences and the likeness between Victorian liberalism and Victorian conservatism, the problem is a formidable one. It is in fact exacerbated by the fact that recent religious history has brought the modern world a good distance—as Arnold foresaw it would—from the Victorian condition, and both terms *conservative* and *liberal* have religious as well as political significances in the relationship between the two men.

If these problems—problems like the assumption of affinity between the attitudes to Newman of Dr. Thomas Arnold and his son, and the disappearance for many of us of the terms *liberal* and *conservative*—are solved, the influence of Newman on Arnold, even accepting that influence is always difficult to establish, is easier to see, and the quality and character of their relationship becomes easier to assess. In a nutshell, Newman is everywhere in Arnold and not only is it not possible somehow magically to detach an element called Newman from Arnold and still retain Arnold integral and whole but Arnold is not possible without Newman. Furthermore, I would insist that, even given (a) the number of other major influences on Arnold, influences like, for example, that of Carlyle's thought, and (b) the obvious differences between the objects the two men were driving at, especially after Newman's conversion to Catholicism, Newman's influence upon Arnold is the major formative influence that shapes not only his thought but also his characteristic ways of presenting it.

A few references to the places and the ways Newman appears in Arnold would be useful. In his essay "The Literary Influence of Academies," also first presented as a lecture at Oxford, Arnold pays another extraordinary tribute to Newman. Here are his words:

> In a production which we have all been reading lately, a production stamped throughout with a literary quality very rare in this country, and of which I shall have a word to say presently—*urbanity*; in this production, the work of a man never to be named by any son of Oxford without sympathy, a man who alone in Oxford of his generation, alone of many generations, conveyed to us in his genius that same charm, that same ineffable sentiment which this exquisite place itself conveys,—I mean Dr. Newman,—an expression is frequently used which is more common in theological than in literary language, but which seems to me fitted to be of general service; the *note* of so and so, the note of catholicity, the note of antiquity, the note of sanctity, and so on. Adopting this expressive word, I say that in the bulk of the intellectual work of a nation which has no centre, no intellectual metropolis like an academy, like M. Sainte-Beuve's "sovereign organ of opinion," like M. Renan's "recognised authority in matters of tone and taste,"—there is observable a *note of provinciality*. Now, to get rid of provinciality is a certain stage of culture; a stage the positive result of which we must not make of too much importance, but which is, nevertheless, indispensable, for it brings us on to the platform where alone the best and highest intellectual work can be said fairly to begin. Work done after men have reached this platform is *classical*; and that is the only work which, in the long run, can stand.[2]

Here the identification between Arnold and Newman is so complete that while on the one hand Arnold praises Newman for his possession of a French-like "urbanity," he uses Newman's manner in the *Apologia* to exemplify the opposite of that provincialism or provinciality which in *Culture and Anarchy*, *Friendship's Garland* and so many other works he ascribes to the English Philistines—the middle class, in power and in love with its own understandings of things. He even looks in the direction of the Sophocles of "Dover Beach," his Homer of the lectures on translating Homer and his Marcus Aurelius of "Pagan and Medieval Religious Sentiment" in affiliating him with classicism and what in *Culture and Anarchy* he calls Hellenism.

Here, in other words, is one of the places in which Arnold once again uses Newman as he tends to use his touchstone figures, to point out the way (to use the phrase Mill applies to the elect in *On Liberty*) and to make clear why the English—and especially the Philistine middle class—need to divest themselves of habits that have become ingrained and tend to threaten to prevent the future from coming into being. His praise of Newman is both of his substance and his style—or perhaps it is better to say that in his praise it is impossible to separate Newman's attitude and posture from the ideas he embraces. Both seem to Arnold invaluable and they are the warp and woof of the same character, manifested in his writings and speaking.

Another reference to the *Apologia* occurs—as we could expect—in *On the Study of Celtic Literature*. Perhaps to make amends for the Achilles reference in "Stanzas from the Grande Chartreuse"—who knows?—Arnold pays Newman a loving tribute as he refers to Eugene O'Curry's *Lectures on the Manuscript Materials of Ancient Irish History*, noting that O'Curry had no "hearer more attentive, more sympathising" than Newman when he delivered them and then, by means of a reference to Newman's use of a line from Lucan's *Pharsalia* in the *Apologia*, he delicately elevates Newman among the immortals once again. He shows his intimate knowledge of the *Apologia* in the way he throws this allusion off but his making use of O'Curry to pay his tribute evinces his inability to pass within even distant sight of Newman without saluting him.

Again, in another place in "The Literary Influence of Academies" Arnold places Newman side by side with Shakespeare as he talks of the difficulty that confronts the

English when they try to divest themselves of the provincial
spirit. Since this passage immediately precedes his careful
distinction between what he calls the "intelligence" in Ruskin and
what he calls—in a very Newmanian way—his "genius," it is of
real importance. Arnold speaks of the need for a "miracle of
genius" like Shakespeare's to produce "balance of mind" and "a
miracle of intellectual delicacy like Dr. Newman's to produce
urbanity of style." The passage seems to echo the distinction
Newman himself makes frequently between the intellect and the
imagination, for example when in *The Tamworth Reading Room*,
Newman distinguishes between the two and asserts, "The heart
is commonly reached, not through the reason, but through the
imagination, by means of direct impressions, by the testimony of
facts and events, by history, by description." When Arnold in
this passage separates the wheat from the chaff in Ruskin, he in
fact offers as a specimen of Ruskin's excellence a passage
descriptive of "the shores of the Swiss lakes."

As these last passages suggest, Newman tends to be invoked
in Arnold as an exemplar not merely of what goals to pursue but
how to conduct oneself so as to ensure some reasonable chance
of attaining those goals. In other words, when he is invoked by
Arnold it is usually in order to comment both on the manner and
the matter of Arnold's discussion, and especially when Arnold is
dealing with the self-consciousness of the English and their
limited objectives and what he calls in "The Study of Poetry"
their materialization of even the most valuable things. Ideas
which are important to Newman are invariably important to
Arnold as well and even though he sometimes takes care to make
distinctions between his understanding and Newman's, he
invariably treads in Newman's footsteps even as he does so. An
excellent example of this is his attack on the materializing
tendencies of English Protestantism in *St. Paul and Protestantism*.
The passage is too long to quote it here, but it occurs in Part II
of the book, in a section called "Puritanism and the Church of
England."

Arnold is talking of one of his favorite subjects, the
protesting and dissenting spirit which has caused so many sects

to arise in Protestantism and such dissension from the Church of England, and begins to focus his ideas by reference to the doctrine of development. It would not in the course of things be necessary in an age in which since Herbert Spencer, ideas of evolutionary change were part of the air one breathed and a constant incitement to the controversial spirit, to invoke Newman but once again Arnold does. Arnold introduces the whole idea in these words: "An admirable writer, in a book which is one of his least known works, but which contains, perhaps, even a greater number of profound and valuable ideas than any other one of them, has set forth, both persuasively and truly, the impression of this sort, which Church-history cannot but convey." He then goes on at great length to quote Newman, referring to *him* by name and to the *Essay on Development* by name and quoting from the Essay three times at some considerable length. When he concludes it is only to invoke Bishop Butler, another of his constant touchstones, and to draw a strong likeness between Butler and Newman. It is easily possible to misread the ending of this passage, however, because in the aftermath of this analogy, Arnold makes one of his several references to Newman's "conclusions," as he calls it, being "at variance with his own principle of development." But this careful reference to Newman's ideas as a Catholic and his movement into the Catholic Church is not *in fact* the end of the passage: it ends with one of Arnold's characteristic sinuous and undulating movements of thought, in which, after his qualifications of his praise of Newman, he returns to Newman and quotes him again, to the effect that "development is not an effect of wishing and resolving, or of forced enthusiasm . . . but comes of its own innate power of expansion within the mind in its season." The effect of this conclusion is to disclaim the disclaimer, more or less to imply that in a book essentially about the heart-wearying tendencies of English Protestantism it would have been difficult not to tilt a lance at Rome but that after all he and Newman are too much of one mind for that tilting of the lance to be anything more than an obligatory ritual gesture.

Putting what I have just said more directly, there are clearly places where Arnold uses the opportunity to refer to Newman, his ideas and his writings, to establish—or seem to establish—some distance between them. But if the lengthy reference in *St. Paul and Protestantism* is any index, this separating of the two is never done with any fullness of heart, is sometimes obviously formulaic, and never undermines the wholeheartedness of the debt that Arnold constantly acknowledges to Newman. In his famous essay "The Bishop and the Philosopher," in which Arnold opposes the ideas of Bishop Colenso to those of another of his touchstones, the Dutch-Jewish philosopher, Spinoza, Newman is again invoked. This time the invoking clearly signifies a writer who has steeped himself in Newman's ideas, who knows his writings intimately, and who has absorbed his ideas and made them his own. The passage is bound to remind us again of *The Tamworth Reading Room*, so let me read it:

The great mass of the human race have to be softened and humanised through their heart and imagination, before any soil can be found in them where knowledge may strike living roots. Until the softening and humanising process is very far advanced, intellectual demonstrations are uninforming for them; and, if they impede the working of influences which advance this softening and humanising process, they are even noxious; they retard their development, they impair the culture of the world. All the great teachers, divine and human, who have ever appeared, have united in proclaiming this. "Remember the covenant of the Highest, and wink at ignorance," says the Son of Sirach. "Unto you," said Christ to a few disciples, "it is given to know the mysteries of the kingdom of heaven, but to them (the multitude) it is not given." "My words," said Pindar, "have a sound only for the wise." Plato interdicted the entry of his school of philosophy to all who had not first undergone the discipline of a severe science. "The vast majority," said Spinoza, "have neither capacity nor leisure to follow speculations." "The few (those who can have a saving knowledge) can never mean the many," says, in one of his noblest sermons, Dr. Newman. Old moral

> ideas leaven and humanise the multitude: new intellectual
> ideas filter slowly down to them from the thinking few; and
> only when they reach them in this manner do they adjust
> themselves to their practice without convulsing it.[3]

Not only does Arnold here echo Newman on the need to touch
the heart and energize the imagination if one hopes to have any
moral effect, or indeed any *lasting* effect, but he accompanies
Newman with such a catalogue of the worthies that even those
who are convinced of the essential difference between Arnold
and Newman must find it difficult to cling to their faith: Christ,
Pindar, the writer of *Ecclesiasticus*, Plato, Spinoza keep company
with Newman here. And indeed Newman appears at the end of
the queue, as if after this no more need be said. Since the idea
being expressed here is one that is essential to Newman's
thought, both as an Anglican and as a Catholic, and since
Newman's idea is used to repudiate the modern "liberal" notion
that advances in theology require the publication of an increasing
number of works like Colenso's, it is clear that Arnold's
invoking of Newman is not a ritual gesture at all, in any way,
this time, but an evidence of the extent to which, when Newman
is brought before the reader in Arnold's writing, he gives
Arnold's opinion and not merely his own (rather as the monks in
the Carthusian monastery speak for him at the end of "Stanzas
from the Grande Chartreuse").

But, as I have indicated, the relationship between Newman
and Arnold, so far as it is a matter of the shadows which the
writings and the sermons of the one throw on the writings and
the lectures of the other, is also important as a matter of style.
Besides the passages I have cited, there are innumerable other
places in Arnold in which Newman is cited as a representative of
the manner and the style to be adopted when dealing with
questions of substance. In *Last Essays on Church and Religion*,
1877, in "A Psychological Parallel," the first of the essays,
Arnold refers, this time without naming the work, to *The Present
Position of Catholics* of 1851 (published in 1857). The ease and
naturalness of the reference again bespeaks familiarity with

Newman's writings, which is this time more remarkable as the work is two decades in the past as Arnold is writing. In this passage Arnold is chiding those he calls "Liberal politicians" for their inability to get rid of the last vestiges of "the system of subscriptions and tests formerly employed so vigorously." He makes another wry gesture in the direction of the things with which they *do* preoccupy themselves, like the Deceased Wife's Sister's Bill, with which he had such fun in *Culture and Anarchy*. And then he introduces Newman's wit in *The Present Position of Catholics*, at the expense of such dullness, referring to it as matter "on which Dr Newman has showered such exquisite raillery." Arnold seems to sigh for Newman, repeating the assertion in *Culture and Anarchy* that grace and wit and elegance rarely have their complete triumph, as he points out that "it is only the Philistine element in our race (which) prevents our seeing the ridiculousness" of what Newman mocks as ridiculous.

In "Our Masses and the Bible," Chapter 10 of *Literature and Dogma*, Arnold again uses the same term *exquisite*, referring this time not to Newman's style merely or a facet of it, like his wit, but to his whole persona, to his whole bearing and demeanor and his handling of his topics, speaking of "this exquisite and delicate genius." Yet even though the reference is broader here than in *Last Essays*, it seems clear enough that it stems from Arnold's enjoyment of and sense of kinship with the stylistic graces, the delicacy of perception, the tact and flexible handling of material which he associates with Newman's treatment of arguments. Certainly the tenor of "exquisite" is re-enforced in the word *delicate* with which Arnold backs it up and the fact that it derives from a partly-aesthetic appreciation of Newman's method is apparent in that.

Aside from those ideas I have mentioned which are common to both writers, and especially those in the discussion of which Arnold alludes to or cites Newman or otherwise makes use of his authority, where in Arnold's ideas can the hand of Newman be seen to write? Certainly in all the enormous enterprise of the castigation of Liberalism (and liberalism) to which Arnold devotes so much time throughout his career. Appendix A of the

Apologia in which Newman presents directly his view of
Liberalism and his justification for opposing it and for feeling
that it opposed him and drove him ultimately to separate from
the Church of England is not the sole origin of Arnold's attitudes
to Liberalism. But one cannot read extensively in both writers
without recognizing that a good deal of Newman underlies
Arnold's saying of himself in the Preface to Culture and
Anarchy, "although like Mr. Bright and Mr. Frederic Harrison,
and the editor of the *Daily Telegraph*, and a large body of friends
of mine, I am a Liberal, yet I am a Liberal tempered by
experience, reflection, and renouncement." This idea of Liberalism tempered—especially by reflection—pervades Arnold's writings on religion and politics particularly but indeed most topics.
It underlies the distinction which he borrows from Newman
between the best self and the ordinary self and which he lays
such stress on in *Culture and Anarchy*, as we all know, but as
some of us do not know, in his religious writings too, for
example in the Preface to *Last Essays*. It underlies the emphasis
he puts, with Newman, on the importance of distancing oneself
from selfishness and which he uses to establish a distinction
between his own position and that of John Stuart Mill.

(For one of several of Newman's statements on this matter,
see Newman's attack on the self-esteem of canting Protestantism
in his sermon on Self-Contemplation of 1835. This is the sermon
in which he uses the image of "derangement" to describe
excessive self-absorption, of the sort which Arnold later ascribes
to English Philistinism and to which he applies such labels as
"smug, self-satisfied." It is interesting to me that in his essay of
1878 condemning his Liberal friends from another point of view,
the essay "Irish Catholicism and British Liberalism," Arnold
himself uses the image of madness to chastise what he calls
Protestant ideas of the power of religion and to stigmatize
"Liberals who have no conception of the Christian religion as of
a real need of the community").

Newman is obviously speaking through Arnold, again, when
Arnold speaks of the power and permanence of Christianity, as
in that same essay on Irish Catholicism, in which Arnold speaks

of the power and permanence coming from "Christianity's being a real source of cure for a real bondage and misery." The question of whether Arnold was or was not a Christian, to put it in its most vulgar form, seems to me as trivialising as the question I raised much earlier, of whether, as the son of a liberal Protestant theologian, Arnold could sympathize with and allow his mind to become captivated by the ideas of the most eminent convert to Catholicism of his day. If one reads Arnold's religious writings with Newman's religious writings in one's mind, one has no difficulty recognizing that the question is a non-starter, that Arnold and Newman share the same faith in the inevitability that Christianity will survive, the same belief in its profound humanising powers, the same idea that it will prove superior to the accommodations that are being made in its name as they write.

At the same time, one of the most interesting of Newman's ideas which surfaces again in Arnold is the idea which Newman puts in section 23 of his sermon "Implicit and Explicit Reason" in these words:

In this point of view we may, without irreverence, speak even of the words of inspired Scripture as imperfect and defective; and though they are not subjects for our judgment (God forbid), yet they still for that very reason serve to enforce and explain better what I would say, and how far the objection goes. Inspiration is defective, not in itself, but in consequence of the medium it uses and the beings it addresses. It uses human language, and it addresses man; and neither can man compass, nor can his hundred tongues utter, the mysteries of the spiritual world, and God's appointments in this. This vast and intricate scene of things cannot be generalized or represented through or to the mind of man; and inspiration, in undertaking to do so, necessarily lowers what is divine to raise what is human. What, for instance, is the mention made in Scripture of the laws of God's government, of His providences, counsels, designs, anger, and repentance, but a gracious mode (the more gracious because necessarily imperfect) of making man contemplate what is far beyond him? Who shall give method to what is infinitely complex, and measure to the unfathomable? We are as worms in an abyss of divine works; myriads upon myriads of years would it take, were our hearts ever so religious, and our intellects ever so apprehensive, to receive from without the just impression of those works as they really are, and as experience would convey them to us:—sooner, then, than we should know nothing, Almighty God has condescended to speak to us so far as human thought and language will admit, by approximations, in order to give us practical rules for our own conduct amid His infinite and eternal operations. (*US*, 268–69)[4]

This idea takes many forms in Arnold, since it is obviously an idea that appeals to him from many sides. For example in the Preface to *Higher Schools and Universities in Germany*, when he condemns Protestantism for its anti-Catholic hysteria and revilings, he tells his Protestant brethren, "it is to our own people and to English Protestantism that we must say, and must use every effort to make the idea intelligible and convincing: 'All forms of religion are but *approximations* to the truth. . . . But all great forms of Christianity are aimed at the truth. . . .' Yet Catholicism we are always looking at from the negative side." Later in the same Preface he presents Catholicism as "tolerable" an approximation as Protestantism, whatever some Protestants prefer to think. In Chapter XI of *Literature and Dogma*, "The True Greatness of the Old Testament," sounding rather more like Newman, he defends popular Christianity against the accusation of being full of errors in the famous passage in which he argues: "The language of the Bible being . . . *approximate*, not scientific, in all expressions of religious feeling approximate language is lawful, and indeed is all we can attain to." But he goes on, "It cannot be adequate, more or less proper it can be; but, in general, approximate language consecrated by use and religious feeling acquires therefrom a propriety of its own." There may be other places in Arnold's writing in which Newman and Arnold grasp hands more firmly than here but in no other, I think, does Arnold himself feel his kinship with Newman more powerfully than here.

These, then, are some of the ways, and I have quoted from some of the places in Arnold that reveal how and why, in which Newman seems to be working with Arnold and where sometimes as a matter of rhetorical strategy but sometimes as a matter of deep conviction, Arnold reveals his indebtedness to Newman. Matters of influence, as I have already said, are difficult to prove and the persuasiveness of the proof depends on the willing acquiescence of the hearer and his familiarity with the same texts. It also depends, in this instance, on his being free of the debilitating tendencies which cripple some criticism—like the tendency I mentioned before of stereotyping Arnold in the image of his father.

Still, to quote a partial sentence myself from one of Newman's sermons, "No analysis is subtle and delicate enough" to indicate "the hues and shades, in which any intellectual view really exists in the mind" and this is obviously as true in the matter of Newman's authority with Arnold as it could be with any subject. But I have left for the last one of the most remarkable of Newman's effects upon Arnold, or so it seems to me. And in referring to it to close, I return in a way to that great passage from "Sweetness and Light" with which I began.

In conducting his campaign on behalf of Culture and in attempting to become a kind of living exemplar of what he calls Criticism, Arnold is forced to confront Protestantism of every stripe and ilk time after time. A devout son of the Church of England himself in his own mind, an apologist for Christianity against the new brand of free-thinkers who saw it as having outlived its utility, a consistent critic of the divisive tendencies Protestantism exhibited as it splintered itself further and further apart with every generation, Arnold is in no doubt about the authenticity of his view of Christianity. In work after work he argues both its acceptability and its necessity.

But what is most remarkable, from one point of view, in his writings on religion and the place (or the way) in which Newman seems to me to be most evident, is in what Arnold has to say about the religion of the future. As I have indicated, he has no doubt that Christianity will survive, despite the dogmatism of those he stigmatizes as Puritans and despite the "progressive" convictions of the new secularists. Yet almost as often as he preaches "the right inculcation of righteousness"[5] or the need to "trust Jesus, whose practice and intuition both of them went . . . so far deeper than ours"[6] or the view that "no other conception of righteousness will do, except Jesus Christ's conception of it:—his method, his secret, and his temper,"[7] he asserts something else. It must have irked his Protestant readers, even those hardened to his reviling of Protestantism and his denunciations of their ethos, to read a passage like this:

> When Ultramontanism, sacerdotalism, and superstition are gone, Catholicism is not, as some may suppose, gone too. Neither is it left with nothing further but what it possesses in common with all the forms of Christianity,—the curative power of the word, character, and influence of Jesus. It is, indeed, left with this, which is the root of the matter, but it is left with a mighty power besides. It is left with the beauty, the richness, the poetry, the infinite charm for the imagination, of its own age-long growth, a growth such as we have described,—unconscious, popular, profoundly rooted, all-encompassing.[8]

Or there is a passage like this, prophesying from the "superiority" of Catholicism: "I persist in thinking that Catholicism has, from this superiority, a great future before it; that it will endure while all the Protestant sects (in which I do not include the Church of England) dissolve and perish. I persist in thinking that the prevailing form for the Christianity of the future will be the form of Catholicism." [9]

And there is a passage like this: "Both Catholic and Protestant have the germ, both Catholic and Protestant have a false philosophy of the germ. But Catholicism has the germ invested in an immense poetry, the gradual work of time and nature, and of that great impersonal artist, Catholic Christendom."[10]

It is in passages like these that Newman's legacy to Arnold

is seen most clearly and the formative influence of Newman's thought upon Arnold's is felt most strongly. There is, in fact, it seems to me, a difference of degree so strong that it amounts almost to a difference of kind between passages like that in *Culture and Anarchy* which assert that the future has been shaped by Newman and the Oxford Movement, or at least it has been saved from being vulgarized, and passages like that which assert that Catholicism is the Christianity of the future. Newman is felt, and a tribute to him is apparent, in both places. But in the passages about the Christianity of the future, in which Arnold writes with warmth and affection of the strengths of Catholicism—what he terms its *poetry*—unperturbed by the incomprehension, the hostility, the dread of middle-class Victorian Protestantism, the influence of Newman is obviously most complete.

Such passages normally contain qualifications of some kind, which I have deliberately omitted to give their main character its full power. But they give an ultimate refinement to Arnold's definition of himself as a Liberal whose Liberalism is tempered by reflection. They reveal that in Arnold Newman's influence is most profoundly felt when it gives to his Liberalism a self-reflective character that Arnold constantly accuses his fellow-Liberals of lacking. And it also gives to it the rhetorical power not only to defeat—usually with "exquisite raillery" such as Newman's —the favorite theorems of the Liberals—what Arnold sometimes calls "our favorite nostrums"—but its most cherished and deeply-fixed biases and antipathies and its most unintelligent but deeply-felt prejudices.

Notes

1. Matthew Arnold, *Culture and Anarchy*, ed. R. H. Super (Ann Arbor: The University of Michigan Press, 1965), 105–7.

2. Matthew Arnold, *Lectures and Essays in Criticism*, ed. R. H. Super (Ann Arbor: The University of Michigan Press, 1973), 244–45.

3. Arnold, *Lectures and Essays in Criticism*, 44.

4. J. H. Newman, "Implicit and Explicit Reason," in *Newman's University Sermons. Fifteen Sermons Preached before the University of Oxford, 1826–43*, with introductory essays by D. M. MacKinnon and J. D. Holmes (London: S.P.C.K., 1970).

5. "The True Greatness of Christianity," section 12, subsection 5, *Literature and Dogma*, in Matthew Arnold, *Dissent and Dogma*, ed., R. H. Super (Ann Arbor: The University of Michigan Press, 1968), 405.

6. Arnold, *Dissent and Dogma*, 404.

7. Arnold, *Dissent and Dogma*, 400.

8. "Irish Catholicism and British Liberalism," in Matthew Arnold, *Mixed Essays*, ed., R. H. Super (Ann Arbor: The University of Michigan Press, 1972), 333.

9. Arnold, *Mixed Essays*, 334.

10. Arnold, *Mixed Essays*, 340.

8
Newman's Catechesis in a Pluralistic Age
Günter Biemer

Two actions in Newman's life reveal his special regard for catechetical instruction both as an Anglican and as a Catholic. At Littlemore he catechized the children, and adults came from Oxford to listen to his talks. One of his first acts when the Oratory was set up in Alcester Street was to begin catechetical lessons in the evening. In this essay I would like to touch upon the source and inspiration of his esteem and practice of catechetical instruction and then to concentrate on what value Newman can be to us engaged in catechetics in a pluralistic society.

1. Historical Sources of Newman's Catechetical Theory and Practice

On "Sunday 1 Febr" 1829 Newman writes in his Diary: I "went to Littlemore in the evening beginning my catechetical lecture" (*LD*, VI, 116; see also 119, 121, 125). In November 1837 we read: "Began catechisings in church" (*LD*, VI, 161).[1] During Lent 1840 Newman wrote in a letter to Jemima: "I am catechising the children in church on Sundays" (*Moz.*, II, 302). One of the visitors reports:

> Newman's catechising has been a great attraction this Lent, and men have gone out of Oxford every sunday to hear it. I heard him last sunday, and thought it very striking, done with much spirit, and the children so up to it, answering with the greatest alacrity. (*Moz.*, II, 302n.1).

The Catechumenate in the Church of the Fathers

The sources of Newman's knowledge about and admiration for Catechesis were his studies of the Early Church, particularly the Church of Alexandria, where he discovered: a significant catechetical system, a significant method interpreting and understanding Scripture, and a special structure of tradition.

In his *Arians of the Fourth Century* (1832/33), Newman described Catechetical instructions according to the Alexandrian School as the pattern of introduction into the Christian Mysteries. The catechumens received "elementary information" as "correct outlines" (*Ari.*, 53) of the Christian message so that they were really "grounding in faith" (*Ari.*, 44). A gradual growth during the catechetical course was usual. They were lead "from the most simple principle of Natural Religion to peculiar doctrines of the Gospel and from moral truth to Christian mysteries" (*Ari.*, 44).[2] Newman learned also that a Christian teacher of this school was expected to have mystagogical qualities for the introduction of the catechumens as well as competency in missionary preaching.

Catechetical teaching and learning was to have an interpersonal atmosphere in order to qualify the participants as witnesses of the Gospel. Newman underlines the following:

> The unfitness of books, compared with private communication, for the purposes of religious instruction; levelling, as they do, the distinctions of mind and temper by the formality of the written character, and conveying each kind of knowledge the less perfectly, in proportion as it is of moral nature, and requires to be treated with delicacy and discrimination. (*Ari.*, 137f.)

Certain concepts such as life, realization, virtue, embodiment are characteristics of what Newman calls *living faith*. He expects the Church to be "decided and plain spoken in its doctrine;" it "must regard faith rather as a character of mind than a notion" (*Ari.*, 147). His old motto that "growth is the only evidence of life," which leads logically to his statement "Knowledge is nothing compared with doing" (*PS*, I, 27), is mirrored in the statement that "arrangements of words . . . have no existence except on paper," while "habits . . . are realities" (*Ari.*, 147).

Summing up we can say: Newman has learned from his study of the Early Church that Catechesis is an instrument of handing on God's Revelation and has its specific laws and criteria: catechesis as a *gradual introduction* starting from Natural Religion leading to the mystery of the Gospel; catechesis as *moral education* leading from moral habits to Christian virtues; catechesis as contribution to the balance between the Apostolic or Episcopal *Tradition* of Creeds (that is, *Oral Tradition*) with the unsystematic statements of revelation in Scripture (Written Tradition); catechesis as *qualification* for the battle between orthodox and heretical representatives; catechesis as a learning process about God's economy so that Christians can identify elements of truth in other philosophical and religious systems within a pluralistic society.

The Basic Principle: Personal Influence

What Newman learned in the study of the Arian Controversy and the history of the councils in the fourth century is for him personalized and concentrated in St. Athanasius (*US*, 97). This is brought out as a structural element for a theory of teaching and learning the faith in his Oxford University Sermon "On personal influence" from January 1832.

This is the red thread of Newman's thought in the Sermon: despite the difficulty of an insufficient human language, a language not adapted for the high task of transmitting God's revelation, and despite the plausibility which the critical faculty of human reason can establish against religious traditions, and despite the great danger of simulation among those who ought to represent and even embody the Gospel—since it is "so easy to be religious on paper"—and despite many other difficulties, error did not prevail in the course of Church history but revelation has been and still is handed down from generation to generation through centuries. "How then after all has it maintained its ground among men?" Newman asks, and the answer is the summary of his sermon:

> I answer that it has been upheld in the world not as a system, not by books, not by argument, nor by temporal power, but by the personal influence of such men (and women) . . . who are at once the teachers and the patterns of it. (*US*, 96, parenthesis added)

Newman's confidence in a faithful teaching and learning the Gospel is based on the fact that those "who are from God" can identify his voice. There is an "attraction, exerted by unconscious holiness, of an urgent and irresistible nature" even over the "thoughtless or perverse multitude," let alone "over that select number . . . who have already in a measure, disciplined their hearts after the law of holiness" (*US*, 85).

Importance of Catechesis for the Catholic Laity

When Newman had become a Roman Catholic he had not only changed from one church to another but also from one social milieu to another. His catechetical activities became adapted to the new requirements as we read about catechetical lectures in the newly opened Oratory in Alcester Street in Birmingham beginning on February 5, 1849 (*LD*, XIII, 26–48).

In the summer of 1851 Newman delivered his "Lectures on the Present Position of Catholics in England addressed to the Brothers of the Oratory." In one of these lectures he gives a vivid description of the contents of adult catechesis when he expects the laity "to enter into their religion, . . . to know their creed, . . . to understand how faith and reason stand out to each other" (*Prepos*, 390).

In 1854, when Newman described his ideal of university learning as an interpersonal encounter he used the learning process of catechesis as a model:

No book can convey the special spirit and delicate peculiarities of its subject with that rapidity and *certainty which attend on the sympathy of mind with mind*, through the eyes, the look, the accent and the manner, in casual expressions thrown off at the moment and the unstudied turns of familiar conversation. . . . The general principle of any study you may learn by books at home; but the details, the color, the tone, the air, the life *which makes it live in us*, you must catch all these from those in whom it lives already. (*HS*, III, 2f.)

This style of learning and teaching Newman goes on to say is meant with catechesis:

It is the living voice, the breathing form, the expressive countenance, . . which catechises. Truth, a subtle, invisible, manyfold spirit, is poured into the mind of the scholar by his eyes and ears, through his affections, imagination and reason; it is poured into his mind and is sealed up there in perpetuity, by propounding, by correcting and explaining, by progressing and than recurring to first principles, by all those ways which are implied in the word "catechising." (*HS*, III, 14f.)

By way of summing up we may say, what catechesis meant to Newman: a communicative acting from person to person in order to acquire a way of life which cannot be taught in books; a living truth, that is, the Gospel, to be learned from those in whom it lives already; with the learning objective of molding the mind upon the Christian Faith; from a process and for a process called Tradition of Revelation.

II. Teaching the Christian Message in a Pluralistic Society

In his book *The Heretical Imperative* Peter L. Berger describes the consequences of modern society for religions. The secular state which is a consequence of the idea of enlightenment admits and even necessitates a plurality of denominations and religions. Secularization is closely connected with the pluralization of the plausibility-structures. Indeed Berger says: "Never before has pluralization of meaning and value systems been experienced so effectively by so many people."[3] The world religions, including Christianity, have to face up to competition and rivalry. They are confronted with the question of how their message can be maintained. With respect to the individual in modern secular society, everybody can and has to make his/her choice. The time when somebody belonged to a denomination by way of family tradition is nearly over.[4]

What are the chances for the Catholic faith in a post-christian society? With that question in mind we come back to Newman's contribution. Newman would certainly not agree with modern schools of sociology of knowledge which consider Christian faith as just one religion among other world religions. But Newman's view of the social reality of his days and the vision of the development of society show a lot of common concerns with modern sociological thought.[5] Three important observations are characteristic for him: the phenomenon of a religion of civilization, the growing enmity against religion in modern society, and the new chances for the Christian faith.

Religion of Civilization

On August 26th 1832 Newman preached on "The Religion of the Day" (*PS*, I, 311–24) which he describes as a selection of the brighter parts of the Christian faith. The representatives of this religion who make use of the consequences of Enlightenment make religion appear as "pleasant and easy":

> Benevolence is the chief virtue; intolerance, bigotry, excess of zeal, are the first sins. Austerity is an absurdity; even firmness is looked on with an unfriendly, suspicious eye. (*PS*, I, 312)

It is a religion which "takes a general colouring from Christianity" (*PS*, I, 313). This religion, he explains,

> is especially adapted to please men of skeptical minds . . .

who have never been careful to obey their conscience, who cultivate the intellect without disciplining the heart, and who allow themselves to speculate freely about what religion ought to be, without going to Scripture to discover what it really is. (*PS*, I, 318)

Newman gives us some very plausible characteristics of that kind of religion:

That we need not alarm ourselves, that God is a merciful God - that amendment is quite sufficient to atone for our offences . . . that the world is, on the whole, very well disposed towards religion, . . . that we should not be overserious, . . . and that we should love all men. This indeed is the creed of shallow men, in every age. (*PS*, I, 319)

And here is Newman's critical evaluation:

That shallowness of religion . . . is the result of a blinded conscience; . . . The fear of God is the beginning of wisdom; till you see him to be a consuming fire and approach him with reverence and godly fear, as being sinners, you are not even in the sight of this straight gate. (*PS*, I, 322)

With the vision of a prophet Newman marked the criteria of a more human than divine religion, of a more liberal than orthodox Christianity, of a more civilized than prophetical and priestly church. And he gives as the reason for this deficient religion a onesided understanding and interpretation of the Christian message, which does not only have a bright side but also a dark one, which is not only a promise but also a judgment and punishment, and requires not only love, but also fear. The two sides of religion remain important for Newman; in his *Grammar of Assent* (1870) he discriminates the true and false understanding on the level of Natural religion:

All religion, so far as it is genuine, is a blessing, Natural as well as Revealed. . . . Its large and deep foundation is the sense of sin and guilt, and without this sense there is for man, as he is, no genuine religion. Otherwise it is but counterfeit and hollow; and that is the reason why this so called religion of civilisation and philosophy is so great a mockery. (*GA*, 258)[6]

From this analysis of *civil religion*, which has not lost its validity, it seems that Newman would insist on a religious instruction which does not only open the horizon for the good tidings in the Bible, but a catechesis which includes a *steady education of the conscience* as the principle of religion and serious introduction to the real mystery of God.

Enmity of Society against Religion

Christian faith in modern society is reflected by Newman also in one of his late papers on "Revelation in its Relation to Faith" (1885). Here he perceives *society as dangerous for religion* in the sense of St. John's understanding of "this world" (kosmos houtos) hoping at the same time that *religion will exercise a critical function in society* and interrupt an upcoming omnipotence of progress in natural sciences and technology.

I say then, that *if*, as I believe, the world, which the Apostles speak of so severely as a False Prophet, is identical with what we call human Society now, then there never was a time since Christianity was when together with the superabundant temporal advantages which by it may come to us, it had the opportunity of being a worse enemy to religion and religious truth than it is likely to be in the years now opening upon mankind. . . . Its conquests in the field of physical science, and its intercommunion of place with place, are a source to it both of pride and of enthusiasm. It has triumphed over time and space; knowledge it has proved to be emphatically power. No problems of the universe, - material, moral, or religious,- are too great for its ambitious essay and its high will to master. There is one obstacle in its path, I mean the province of religion. But can religion hope to be successful? (*TP*, I, 145)[7]

Is it a stern vision which Newman takes with respect to position of religion in modern society? The important point for teaching and learning the Gospel is that Newman insists on the discrimination between the world's understanding of religion and the way in which Christians themselves have to understand their faith. Newman is fighting against the "usurpations of reason" in the realm of religion, against liberalism in other words. He is watchful not pessimistic:

> Not, of course, that I suppose, that the flood of unbelief will pour over us in its fullness at once. A large inundation requires a sufficient time, and there are always in the worst times witnesses for the truth to stop the plague. (*TP*, I, 145)

Here Newman may have in mind the result of his research in the history of salvation that "our Athanasius and Basil will be given us in their destined season to break the bonds of the Oppressor, and let the captives go free" (*Ari.*, 394).

New Chances for Religion

In his university discourse "A Form of Infidelity of the Day" (1854) Newman speaks of the "open development of unbelief in Germany" and "its growing audacity in England" and says that "unbelief is in some shape unavoidable in an age of intellect" (*Idea*, 310).[8] He stresses the great advantage of such a situation:

> (If) unbelief speaks out that Faith can speak out too, that if falsehood assails Truth, Truth can assail falsehood. In such an age it is possible to found a university more emphatically Catholic than could be set up in the middle age, because Truth can entrench itself carefully, and define its own profession severely, and display its colours unequivocally, by occasion of that very unbelief which so shamelessly vaunts itself. (*Idea*, 311)

This seems a necessary attitude according to Newman in an

age of open infidelity because Christians in such a society will have to face certain schools of philosophy and certain schools of natural sciences which expect the results of their thought and research to prove one day the untenableness of the Christian message, to falsify its traditions and contents, and to demonstrate scientifically that there is nothing except the material world.

III. Didactic Outlines for Catechesis

What are the main topics of catechesis for Christians in a pluralistic society according to Newman? It is certainly not possible to give more than a short survey of those items which mark the specific content of Christian faith in a time of outward crisis in society and of necessary, inner reforms in the church.

Newman finishes his article "On Consulting the faithful in matters of doctrine" from 1859 with the comprehensive statement:

> I think certainly, that the ecclesia docens is more happy when she has . . . enthusiastic partisans about her . . . than when she cuts off the faithful from the body of her divine doctrines and the sympathy of her divine contemplations, and requires from them a fides implicita in her word, which in the educated classes will terminate in indifference, and in the poor in superstition. (*Cons.*, 106)[9]

It is in this context that one has to see Newman's own vocation in the Catholic Church as he understood it:

> To aim then at improving the condition, the status, of the Catholic body by a careful survey of their argumentative basis, of their position relatively to the philosophy and the character of the day, by giving them juster views, by enlarging and refining their minds, in one word, by education. (*A W*, 259)

He wrote this rendering his own account before the eyes of God in his journal in the birthday entry on January 21, 1863. And in a sort of summary he continues: "Now from first to last, education, in this large sense of the word, has been my line" (*A W*, 259).

For didactics of catechesis in pluralistic society Newman suggests six elements:

Criteria of Methodological Consequence for Catechesis

Since God's revelation is *a living truth*, "the life which makes it live in us" must be caught "from those in whom it lives already" (*HS*, III, 9); since God's revelation has its center in the incarnation, the *incarnational method*[10] is the only adequate method of passing on the divine truth from generation to generation; teaching and learning the Christian faith is first of all an effect of God's grace, but since it is also a human process it has its own laws of *gradual growth* from Natural Religion to the Christian mysteries, from implicitness to explicitness.

Conditions of Teaching and Learning the Faith

Everybody has his/her presuppositions of thinking, the *"first principles"* of which one is seldom completely aware—they should be the starting points of involvement for the "venture of faith"; the *moral status* is an important help or obstacle on the way of entering into the Christian truth as Newman observes, "the rejection of Christianity to arise from a fault of the *heart*, not of the *intellect*; that unbelief arises not from mere error of reasoning, but either from pride or from sensuality" (*LD*, I, 219);[11] the *acquisition of the truth* in the cognitive domain is different from that in the existential domain—in Newman's terms a real proposition is necessary in order to effect a real apprehension and a real assent (this goes together with the criterion of handing on a living truth).

The *Contents of Teaching and Learning* the Christian Faith

In the dimension of Natural Religion the development of

conscience is of basic importance since conscience as the sense of duty "is the creative principle of religion, as the moral sense is the principle of ethics" (*GA*, 76); to make the *Creed* the guideline of religious instruction has been proved useful through the centuries of Christianity provided this kind of Apostolic or Episcopal Tradition will be connected with reading Holy Scripture where the truths of Christianity are contained in a more unsystematic but living shape; since "incarnation (is) the central truth of the Gospel, and the source whence we are to draw out its principles" (*Dev.*, 324) catechesis has to have its *focus in Jesus Christ*—to put it in a more operational way, teaching and preaching is the instrument that Jesus Christ uses "to imprint the Image or idea of himself in the minds of his subjects individually; and that Image, apprehended and worshipped in individual minds, becomes a principle of association and a real bond of those subjects one with another" (*GA*, 298f.); nor is Newman content with the incarnational principle in the sense of the Christmas mystery—the incarnational principle includes the paschal mystery, "the cross as the measure of the world,"[12] so that catechetical instruction should include an introduction into the liturgical year as a possibility to live out the mystery of Christ and of salvation history in the annual cycles of one's life.

The *Teachers of Catechesis*

These teachers are of central importance. They should lead their fellow Christians in learning processes gradually on to the fullness of the original destiny, since,

> each of us has the prerogative of completing his inchoate and rudimental nature, and of developing his own perfection out of the living elements with which his mind began to be. It is his gift to be the creator of his own sufficiency; and to be emphatically self-made. (*GA*, 225)

The teachers and preachers have to be the "patterns" of the Gospel-message (*US*, 92), and in due turn each Christian has the mission to be a witness of the Gospel truth. In an elementary way Newman says in his sermon "On the Infidelity of the Future" of October 2nd 1873:

> Any child well instructed in the catechism, is, without intending it, a real missionary. And why? Because the world is full of doubtings and uncertainty, and of inconsistent doctrine - a clear consistent idea of revealed truth, on the contrary, cannot be found outside of the Catholic church. Consistency, completeness is a persuasive argument for a system being true.[13]

Learning Objectives in Curriculum Discussion

According to Newman, what then are the learning objectives of catechesis, which is one of the key term in curriculum discussion? The laity should be enabled to be "the measure of the Catholic spirit" today as it was in all times; Catholics should know their "religion so perfectly, as to be able to volunteer a defence of it" (*Prepos.*, 390); it is not sufficient to reach only cognitive objectives, but sound learning will be "a work of long time; months, sometimes years, . . . devoted to the arduous task of disabusing the mind of the Christian of its pagan (materialistic, hedonistic, egoistic) errors and of *molding it upon the Christian faith*" (*Prepos ,* preface; parenthesis added); to qualify each Christian has to become "one of the myriads of the faithful, none of them known to fame, who received . . . and transmitted so faithfully, generation after generation, the once delivered Apostolic faith; who held it with such sharpness of outline and explicitness of detail as enabled even the unlearned instinctively to discriminate between truth and error" (*HS*, III, 14f.); to make the "Ventures of Faith" a lifelong process in which the relation between "myself and my creator" is growing in intensity because "growth is the only evidence of life" and the mystery of the living God is greater than any image of him in human categories.[14]

Stages of Faith

One of the most recent developments in theories of religious learning shows that there are "Stages of Faith"[15] and "Steps of Religious Development" in human life. There is no doubt that these observations of a steady process in our relationship to God are a valuable help to understand teaching and learning the Gospel truth. On the other hand it would be interesting and highly inspiring to introduce Newman's steps of his own faith development in order to show critically that those stages of faith do not lead further in the seasons of Newman's life than to his first conversion in 1816 or to his religious experience in Sicily in 1833.[16] In other words, what James Fowler calls "conjunctive faith" (stage 5) or Fritz Oser calls autonomy of the person in agreement with the apriori acceptance of Providence (stage 4) are not the highest or last scores in a man's and woman's growth to the mystery of God according to Newman. His further spiritual growth after 1833 shows several developmental stages, for example, in his relationship to the church as God's instrument of salvation during his Anglican time and during his Catholic time, his description of the "History of Religious Opinions" (1864) in the light of God's Providence.[17]

Conclusion

There is a great break to be observed nowadays in the continuity of religious tradition in our church. And though there may be many reasons to account for that, one of the important factors could be a *deficient catechesis*. At least according to Newman there is a close relationship between catechesis and the qualification of the faithful for handing on the faith in the church. Tradition, he says,

> is not a sample or specimen of us merely, but it is we, our thinking, speaking, acting self; our principles, our judgements, our proceedings. What we hold, what we do not hold, what we like, what we hate . . . What is called painting from the

life. (*Prepos*, 326)

Catechesis is or should be the gradual introduction into this living atmosphere of Christian truth through witnesses, who are "at once teachers and patterns of it" giving the possibility "to learn life from those in whom it lives already," "attending on the sympathy of mind with mind," leading from Natural Religion to Revelation and "from moral truth to the Christian mysteries," qualifying the Christians under the guidance of the Holy Spirit to give themselves public testimony of God's overruling Providence which is working mysteriously in the history of humankind. Catechesis is such a thorough introduction to the knowledge and practice of faith, hope and charity that Christians perdure "the course of their trial," the time of their affliction so that they may experience the hour when "slow-paced truth overtakes" "the powers of the world, its counsels and its efforts" (*US*, 94). Newman's understanding of catechetical instruction is surely an ideal taken from his studies of the Alexandrian church, but his understanding does not take its appeal to historical reality, it rather confirms and proves it. Such a catechesis will lead to the hope which the young Oxford scholar expressed at the end of his *Arians of the Fourth Century*, that "our Athanasius and Basil will be given us in their destined season to break the bonds of the Oppressors and let the captives go free" (*Ari.*, 394).

Notes

1. Newman "began catechising children (!) in Church, " (*Letters and Correspondence of John Henry Newman During His Life in the English Church*, ed. Anne Mozley, 2 vols. [London, 1891], II, 248).

2. For this connection of "The Analogy of Religion, Natural and Revealed" Newman was prepared from J. Butler's book (1736) which he read between 1823–25 (*Apo.*, 22f., and *John Henry Newman. Autobiographical Writings*, ed. Henry Tristram [London, 1957], 78).

3. P. L. Berger, *The Heretical Imperative: Contemporary*

Possibilities of Religious Affirmation (Garden City, NY: Doubleday, 1979), German Edition, *Zwang zur Häresie* (Frankfurt: S. Fischer, 1980), 37.

4. P. L. Berger, T. Luckmann, *The Social Construction of Reality. A Treatise in the Sociology of Knowledge* (Garden City, NY: Doubleday, 1966). One may certainly ask whether Berger's paradigm of making a decision for one religious system or the other is legitimately called an "heretical imperative" or whether this term is not simply estranged or perverted. And in addition the author of *The Social Construction of Reality* can surely be asked whether his model of decision-making takes those many anonymous powers into account which influence the individual in a modern mass-media society, in a society of advertisement and consumption.

5. See my article, "Religious Education—A Task between Divergent Plausibilities," on John Henry Newman's contribution towards a modern theory of religious education, in, H. Jenkins, ed., *Newman and Modernism. Newman Studien*, vol. XIV (Sigmaringendorf: Regio Verlag Glock & Lutz, 1990).

6. John Henry Newman, *An Essay in Aid of a Grammar of Assent* (1870), edited, introduction, and notes by I. T. Ker (Oxford: Clarendon Press, 1986).

7. *The Theological Papers of John Henry Newman on Faith and Certainty*, vol. I, ed. Hugo M. de Achaval, J. Derek Holmes (Oxford: Clarendon Press, 1976).

8. John Henry Newman, *The Idea of a University* (1873), edited with introduction and notes by I. T. Ker (Oxford: Clarendon Press, 1976).

9. John Henry Newman, *On Consulting the Faithful in Matters of Doctrine* (1859), edited with an introduction by John Coulson, based on the 1871 revised edition (London: Geoffrey Chapman, 1961).

10. John Coulson, *Religion and Imagination* (Oxford: Clarendon Press, 1981), 59.

11. Letter to Charles Newman from 24 March, 1825.

12. See Newman's sermon "The Cross of Christ the measure of the world" from 9 April, 1841, in *PS*, VI, 83–90.

13. *Catholic Sermons of Cardinal Newman*, published from Newman's manuscripts and edited at the Birmingham Oratory (London: Burns and Oates, 1957), 113.

14. See Newman's sermon "Ventures of Faith" from 21 February, 1836, in *PS*, IV, 295–306, and *Apo.*, 4f.

15. See J. Fowler, S. Kean, *Life-maps. Conversations on the Journey of Faith* (Texas: Word Books, 1978); J. Fowler, *Faith Development and Pastoral Care* (Philadelphia: Fortress Press, 1987); K. E. Nipkow, F. Schweitzer, J. Fowler, *Glaubensentwicklung und Erziehung* (Gütersloh: Gütersloher Verlagshaus Gerd Mohn, 1989); F. Oser, P. Gmünder, *Der Mensch-Stufen seiner religiosen Entwicklung. Ein strukturgenetischer Ansatz* (Zurich: Benzinger, 1984); F. Oser, *Wieviel Religion braucht der Mensch? Erziehung und Entwicklung zur religiösen Autonomie* (Gütersloh: Gütersloher Verlagshaus Gerd Mohn, 1988).

16. See my article "Stufen des Glaubens. Newmans Treue zur inneren Stimme", in G. Greshake, ed., *Gottes Word-Antwort des Menschen* (Würzburg: Echter, 1991).

17. It is remarkable that E. H. Erikson's studies on the life-cycle extend until old age, see E. H. Erikson, "The Problem of ego-identity," in *The Journal of the American Psycho-analytical Association* 1956, and later reprints; German edition, E. H. Erikson, *Identität und Lebenszyklus* (Frankfurt: Suhrkamp, 1966), 123–212, and see the critical evaluation by G. Moran in, *Religious Education Development. Images for the Future* (Minneapolis, MN: Winston Press, 1983), especially his six "moments" according to Kieran Egan, *Educational Development* (New York: Oxford University Press, 1979).

9

Newman's Advice to Victims of Anti-Catholic Prejudice
Jay Newman

John Henry Newman's 1851 Birmingham Corn Exchange lectures on *The Present Position of Catholics in England* were delivered at a particularly hard time for English Catholics. Hostility toward English Catholics had increased dramatically in 1850 as a response to measures restoring the Catholic hierarchy. Newman gave his fellow English Catholics this assessment of the situation:

> Bear in mind, then, that, as far as defamation and railing go, your enemies have done their worst. There is nothing which they have not said, which they do not daily say, against your religion, your priests, and yourselves. They have exhausted all their weapons and you have nothing to fear, for you have nothing to lose. They call your priests distinctly liars: they can but cry the old fables over and over again, though they are sadly worse for wear. They have put you beyond the pale of civilized society; they have made you the outlaws of public opinion; they treat you, in the way of reproach and slander, worse than they treat the convict or the savage. (*Prepos.*, sec. 3)[1]

Newman classified these enemies into four main categories: "First, a great proportion of members of both Houses of Parliament; next, the press; thirdly, the Societies whose haunt or home is Exeter Hall; fourthly, the pulpits of the Establishment, and of a good part of the Dissenters."

In the Corn Exchange lectures, Newman countered the anti-

Catholic campaigns in several ways. He offered insights into the
nature of prejudice, directly attacked the charges of the slan-
derers, and provided encouragement to the frightened. He also
recommended what he described as a "defensive system"
(*Prepos.*, sec. 4), a strategy of response to religious prejudice, and
it is this particular dimension of his project to which I shall now
turn.

What was Newman's strategy? Was it sound? Did Newman
give his fellow Catholics good advice? And most importantly,
what, if anything, can today's victims of religious prejudice,
Catholics and non-Catholics alike, learn from the relevant
reflections of this celebrated Christian thinker?

I. Newman's Defensive System

"And now," he asks, "what are our duties at this moment
towards this enemy of ours?"

> Protestantism is fierce, because it does not know you;
> ignorance is its strength; error is its life. Therefore bring
> yourselves before it, press yourselves upon it, force yourselves
> into notice against its will. Oblige men to know you;
> persuade them, importune them, shame them into knowing
> you. Make it so clear what you are that they cannot affect not
> to see you, nor refuse to justify you. Do not even let them
> off with silence, but give them no escape from confessing that
> you are not what they have thought you were. . . . You have
> but to aim at making men look steadily at you; when they do
> this, I do not say they will become Catholics, but they will
> cease to have the means of making you a by-word and a
> reproach, of inflicting on you the cross of unpopularity.
> Wherever Catholicism is known, it is respected, or at least
> endured, by the people. Politicians and philosophers, and the
> established clergy, would be against you, but not the people,
> if it knew you. . . . Your one and almost sole object, I say,
> must be to make yourselves known.

Newman warns that he is not advocating anything rude,

turbulent, or offensive; but he also insists that it is dangerous for Birmingham Catholics to strive to maintain a low profile:

> (Your enemies) have thought not only that you were the vilest and basest of men, but that you were fully conscious of it yourselves, and conscious, too, that they knew it. They have fancied that you, or at least your priests, . . . dared not look a Protestant in the face. Accordingly, they have considered, and have thought us quite aware ourselves, that we were like reputed thieves and other bad characters, who, for one reason or another, are not molested in their dens of wickedness, and enjoy a contemptuous toleration, if they keep within bounds. And so, in like manner, they have thought that there was evidence enough at any moment to convict us, if they were provoked to it. What would be their astonishment if one of the infamous persons I have supposed stood upon his rights, or obtruded himself into the haunts of fashion and good breeding? (*Prepos.*, secs. 1–2)

Newman has here identified a potential weakness of many traditional responses to religious prejudice. The concept of prejudice is epistemological; the prejudiced person pre-judges, or judges in ignorance. The cure for ignorance is enlightenment, education, the dissemination of knowledge, and the presentation of evidence. When one has direct contact with Catholics or members of other religious minorities, one can perhaps see for oneself that these people are not nearly as terrible as bigots and hatemongers have made them out to be. Yet many victims of religious prejudice adopt a defensive strategy of *withdrawal*. Assuming, or at least hoping, that prejudice will eventually disappear by itself, they decide to keep a low profile and to avoid rocking the boat. But religious prejudice rarely disappears by itself. And when the member of a religious minority voluntarily withdraws into a ghetto and avoids making personal contacts with members of the religious majority, she makes it easier for the ignorance or pre-judgment to flourish. Enlightened people will conclude that, "These people are decent, conciliatory folks who mind their own business." But others may conclude

that, "These outsiders know their place; surely they have plenty
to hide." Those who isolate themselves from their fellow citizens
should not be surprised when they learn that these fellow citizens
have never ceased harboring mistaken ideas about them. Is it not
safer then for the member of a religious minority to have the
courage of her convictions and come out in the open? Should
she not show her neighbors that she has nothing to hide and
nothing of which to be ashamed? And should she not also show
them that she is not aloof and that she values their
companionship? Newman insists that his fellow English Catholics
have nothing to lose: "Whatever occurs, if there be a change at
all, it must be a change for the better; you cannot be
disadvantaged by the most atrocious charges, for you are sure to
be the objects of such, whatever you do" (*Prepos.*, sec. 3).

Newman's second piece of advice to local Catholics is that
they should concentrate their attention on concrete, personal,
local contacts:

> Never mind the London press; never mind Exeter Hall; never
> mind perambulating orators or solemn meetings; let them
> alone, they do not affect local opinion. . . . Look at home,
> there lies your work; what you have to do, and what you can
> do, are one and the same. Prove to the people of Birmingham,
> as you can prove to them, that your priests and yourselves are
> not without conscience, or honour, or morality. . . .
>
>   Let the London press alone; do not appeal to it; do not
> expostulate with it; do not flatter it; care not for public
> opinion, cultivate local. And then if troubled times come on,
> and the enemy rages, . . . the Birmingham people will say,
> "Catholics are, doubtless, an infamous set, and not to be
> trusted, for the *Times* says so, and Exeter Hall, and the Prime
> Minister, and the Bishops of the Establishment; and such good
> authorities cannot be wrong; but somehow an exception must
> certainly be made for the Catholics of Birmingham." And in
> like manner, the Manchester people will say, "Oh, certainly,
> Popery is horrible, and must be kept down. Still, let us give
> the devil his due, they are a remarkably excellent body of men
> here." And thus, my Brothers, the charges against Catholics

will become a sort of Hunt-the-slipper, everywhere and nowhere, and will end in "sound and fury, signifying nothing." (*Prepos.*, secs. 3–4)

One of the central themes of Newman's philosophy is that the concrete and personal is far more important than the abstract and impersonal; much of his work consists of practical applications of this empiricist principle, and here again we see him putting it to practical use. Too many victims of prejudice respond by tilting at windmills, jousting with abstractions on unfamiliar ground. Rather than wasting time and effort combatting hidden, unseen enemies, these people should be working to make friends at home.

> Newman next warns his co-religionists to beware of parties: You are attacked on many sides; do not look about for friends on the right or on the left. Trust neither Assyria nor Egypt; trust no body of men. Fall back on yourselves, and trust none but yourselves. I do not mean you must not be grateful to individuals who are generous to you, but beware of parties; all parties are your enemies; beware of alliances. (*Prepos.*, sec. 4)

Here it is the student of politics speaking. It is hard for the victim of prejudice to avoid the temptation to seek the support of powerful groups: political parties, labour unions, business groups, academic societies, and so forth. Temporary gains will be made by entering into such alliances; but a price will have to be paid. The victim of prejudice must buy the good will of his ally, either with votes, money, or long-range commitments. To help one party is to risk incurring the resentment of opposition parties. If you work closely with the political left, you may alienate the political right. If you look to organized labour as your friend, you can no longer expect a fair hearing from the captains of industry. Moreover, when your "friends" no longer need you, or have reason to take your support for granted, they will dump you without a moment's hesitation. Is it not more prudent then to deal with human beings as individuals rather than make deals with parties or groups?

Newman next speaks of the importance of an educated laity. Here we hear the voice of the author of *The Idea of a University* and "On Consulting the Faithful":

> You must not hide your talent in a napkin, or your light under a bushel. I want a laity, not arrogant, not rash in speech, not disputatious, but men who know their religion, who enter into it, who know just where they stand, who know what they hold and what they do not, who know their creed so well that they can give an account of it, who know so much of history that they can defend it. . . . You ought to be able to bring out what you feel and what you mean, as well as to feel and mean it; to expose to the comprehension of others the fictions and fallacies of your opponents; and to explain the charges brought against the Church, to the satisfaction, not, indeed, of bigots, but of men of sense, of whatever cast of opinion. And one immediate effect of your being able to do all this will be your gaining that proper confidence in self which is so necessary for you. (*Prepos.*, sec. 4)

Every individual Catholic, or Jew or Sikh or Presbyterian, is an ambassador for her denomination. If she does not understand her own religion, how can she expect outsiders to understand it? And how can she reply intelligently to those who make unfair criticisms of it? The member of a religious minority cannot afford simply to take consolation in the fact that somewhere in her religious community there are learned people who can refute the hatemonger's claims. She must know pretty well where she and her co-religionists stand. For if she does not, she will make her hostile critics look more knowledgeable than they are, and she may herself slip into unwarranted self-contempt.

Newman's fifth point concerns the importance of strong personal qualities:

> Your opponents, my Brothers, are too often emphatically *not* gentlemen: but it will be for you, in spite of whatever provocations you may meet with, to be manly and noble in

your bearing towards them; to be straightforward in your dealings with them; to show candour, generosity, honourable feeling, good sense, and forbearance, in spite of provocation; to refrain from taking unfair or small advantages over them; to meet them half way, if they show relentings; not to fret at insults, to bear imputations, and to interpret the actions of all in the best sense you possibly can.   It is not only more religious, not only more becoming, not only happier, to have these excellent dispositions of mind, but it is far the most likely way, in the long run, to persuade and succeed. (*Prepos.*, sec. 5)

Being virtuous, being a "gentleman," is not only moral and Christian but generally prudent as well. A Roman Catholic must be noble and generous in spite of the provocations he meets. But are nobility and generosity always prudent? Is Newman not advocating in many cases a great deal of sacrifice, even martyrdom? To some extent he is, and that is his sixth and final point. "Not every age is the age of Saints, but no age is not the age of Martyrs" (*Prepos.*, sec. 6). "Let them exterminate us, as they have done before, kill the priests, decimate the laity; and they have for a while defeated the Pope. They have no other way; they may gain a material victory, never a moral one" (*Prepos.*, sec. 6).

Here then is Newman's "defensive system," his outline of a strategy of response to at least a certain kind of religious prejudice.   He is recommending it to nineteenth-century Birmingham Catholics, but some of his ideas have a broader application and a continuing relevance.

II. Some Critical Observations

Newman's celebrated rhetorical talents are so imposing that almost anything he says has initial plausibility.   But after considering his six recommendations closely, we can see that there are serious weaknesses in his "defensive system."

There is a serious inconsistency in Newman's analysis.   In

defending his claim that his co-religionists should not keep a low profile, Newman says that they have nothing to lose: "Your enemies have done their worst;" "If there be a change at all, it must be a change for the better." Newman himself, however, has second thoughts on this matter:

> Yet I confess I have not that confidence on the subject which I had a year since, when I said that Catholics never could be persecuted again in England. It will not be so: yet late events have shown, that though I have never underrated the intense prejudice which prevails against us, I did overrate that Anglo-Saxon love of justice and fair dealing which I thought would be its match. (*Prepos.*, sec. 5)

If responding boldly to prejudice can lead to more serious prejudice and even persecution, then the prudence of abandoning a painstakingly cultivated unobtrusiveness is at least questionable. Though English Catholics in 1851 were clearly victims of prejudice and abuse, their situation could have been much worse. As an authority of sorts on Christian martyrdom, Newman was well aware of the depths to which bigots can sink. The contemporary observer can see that in many parts of the globe, murder, torture, and harassment of members of religious minorities are still routine practices. He can see that it is possible for a nation that produced a Beethoven and a Goethe to produce a Himmler and a Streicher, just as the church that produced a Thomas More produced a Torquemada. How many people can reasonably and confidently predict that no matter what course of action they take, their situation cannot possibly get worse? It is only those whose situation is so hopeless that responding aggressively in Newman's sense is not even a viable option. Newman's second thoughts then are certainly justified, and it is troubling that he did not appreciate the degree to which they invalidate his first piece of advice.

We must also question Newman's assumption that direct contact is invariably a cure for prejudice. Some of the worst anti-Catholics and anti-Semites, for example, have been people who have had considerable personal contact with Catholics and Jews in everyday life; and some of the most tolerant people have been people who have had little or no contact with members of persecuted minorities. Do we not, alas, often hear hatemongers tell "innocents" that, "If you knew these people as well as I do, you too would mistrust them"? Newman writes, "Wherever Catholicism is known, it is respected, or at least endured, by the people" (*Prepos.*, secs. 1–2). The plausibility of this claim, however, depends on how one interprets the terms *known* and *endured*.

Newman certainly gives no indication that he properly appreciates the extent to which nineteenth-century criticisms of the Catholic church were fair and reasonable. Contemporary Catholic historians, for example, often allow that nineteenth-century Catholic leaders, including Newman himself, were not as tactful or understanding as they might have been in their dealings with non-Catholics. Their defenses of the Catholic faith were often combined with crude, inaccurate, and unwarranted attacks on Protestantism, Judaism, Islam, liberalism, and other creeds and ways of life. And though anti-Catholics like Giacinto Achilli were often liars, they often had first-hand knowledge of some of the Catholic church's darker, more troubling institutions and policies. Personal contact is ordinarily valuable to the extent that the victim of prejudice indeed has nothing to hide; but the Birmingham Catholics of Newman's age understandably had difficulty divesting themselves of the negative aspects of their association with an institution that was rightly perceived as being egregiously intolerant in its own right.

Newman rightly attaches importance to direct personal contacts. If members of the religious majority see that the Catholic or Jew or liberal atheist is capable of being a gentleman, of being noble and generous and honourable—as he indeed is—they will certainly think the better of him and may even reconsider their negative views about "the Catholics" or "the Jews" or "the atheists." But Newman has committed the fallacy of all-or-nothing. He may have been right in believing that Victorian Catholics had devoted a disproportionate amount of attention to the anti-Catholic diatribes of the London press, the politicians, the Anglican bishops, and others. But why ignore them? The victim of prejudice can, and should, respond on several levels. As important as direct personal contact is, it cannot completely negate the influence of widely disseminated propaganda. Newman undervalues the influence of people in high places. A general weakness of his philosophy is that, in the empiricist tradition, he overemphasizes the concrete and perceptual at the expense of the abstract and conceptual. "Notions" are often more impressive than perceptions. Impersonal contacts should not be allowed to replace personal ones, as they are not effective substitutes; but they should be combined with personal ones, as they have their own special value. Certainly Newman is naive when he suggests that London opinion does not affect local opinion.

Newman has overstated his second point in another way. "Look at home, there lies your work." But are we not our brother's keeper? If members of a denomination are prospering in one area, should they then be unconcerned about the persecution of their co-religionists in another? If Catholics are being harassed in England, is this not appropriately a matter of concern to Catholics in Italy and France? Newman believes that the good will of Protestants in Birmingham and Manchester will spread to the point where "the charges against Catholics will become a sort of Hunt-the-slipper." But bad will spreads too, and prudence dictates that no pocket of prejudice and hatred be allowed to flourish. Moreover, if Protestants in Birmingham sincerely believe that Catholics are an "infamous set" and that the Catholics in Birmingham are, for some mysterious and inexplicable reason, exceptions to the rule, it will be easy for them and their progeny to lapse back into hostility toward their Catholic neighbors in Birmingham. Newman then is unwisely fatalistic on two scores. He wrongly believes that it is impossible to influence "public" (as opposed to local) opinion; and he wrongly believes that it is impossible to lead local non-Catholics to look favorably upon the Catholics of another area. Some of his expectations are extremely narrow.

When Newman warns his co-religionists to beware of alliances, he is talking as a political realist of sorts. But how perceptive a student of politics is he being here? He is surely overstating the point when he tells his fellow Catholics that all parties are their *enemies*. Realism is one thing, but cynicism is another. There are progressive leaders and reactionary ones, and likewise progressive and reactionary parties. In spite of its many weaknesses, the democratic system of government is probably a good deal better than any of the realistically available alternatives. Political maneuvering can be risky and demeaning, but in a democratic system, one either learns to make use of the means of influence open to one or resigns oneself to having no voice in a key phase of political decision-making. And there is power in numbers; it is not without reason that people enter into such interest groups as labour unions, professional associations, fraternal societies, political parties, and communities of believers. Though leaders of interest groups should be cautious in their political maneuvering, they should take advantage of all powers open to them; and if interest groups utilize their political powers intelligently and efficiently, then even their most callous and calculating allies will be reluctant, even afraid, to desert them. So Newman has again overstated his point. It is prudent to recognize that one's political allies are not necessarily friends; but enlightened political allies *can* be friends, and in any case, potential political allies are not necessarily ":enemies." Newman's third piece of advice to his co-religionists has anti-democratic overtones, for he is telling them, in effect, to give up on an inherently corrupt political system. Newman's views on democracy were, in fact, rather ambivalent and underwent much transformation over the years.

In any case, the Roman Catholics of Victorian England constituted a minority. Newman may well have hoped that Anglicans would soon come to their senses, join the True Fold, institute a Catholic theocracy in England, and suppress the wicked apostates, "liberals," and outsiders. But the people of England had quite different ideas, so English Catholics could hardly afford to follow Newman's advice and opt to withdraw from the political system.

Newman's fourth and fifth points are both pertinent and profound. Every person should know her creed so well that she can give an account of it and defend it; one should be able to bring out what one feels and means, as well as feel and mean it. Every person should be noble and straightforward in his dealings with other people, whether they are his co-religionists or not. Everyone should strive to be a virtuous and civilized human being. It is both prudent and good in more profound ways to have virtuous dispositions; and for the member of a minority group, it is usually all the more prudent. Even on this point, however, I have two reservations. Newman has wisely warned his fellows to avoid being arrogant, disputatious, and rash in speech; and he has wisely recommended to them that they know where they stand so that they can defend their faith. In the same place, however, he has also advised them to know "where lie the main inconsistencies and absurdities of the Protestant theory" (*Prepos.*, sec. 4). Now a Catholic ought to know why he rejects Protestantism, just as a Jew or Protestant ought to know why he rejects Catholicism or Islam. And one ought to be able to defend one's faith, at least on some level. Moreover, Newman is right to remind us that a Catholic cannot be a relativist who believes that other people's religions are as good as her own. But it is imprudent and often immoral in a more profound way for a member of a religious minority to attack the religion of the majority as a mass of absurdities. It is one thing to believe, or even know, that another person's religious outlook is riddled with inconsistencies; it is quite another to point the fact out to him by way of a supposed "defense" of one's own faith. Even when one's own religious beliefs have been attacked, it is not always wise to counterattack. Defense and counterattack involve two different motives and two different (if ordinarily associated) strategies. Every person, no matter what his creed, has at least a trace of the missionary in him. Newman, of course, was a great proselytizer, a great witness for his faith. Whether or not religious proselytizing is always morally acceptable, however, it is not necessarily tied to self-defense.

I have already articulated my second reservation: it may not be prudent to be a gentleman in all situations. Perhaps there are some imputations that we ought not to bear, and some provocations that we ought not to ignore. Perhaps Newman is too quick in places to encourage sacrifice and martyrdom. Newman has not advised his Catholic fellows to rush to martyrdom. He has encouraged them to fight back. But he does devote a large proportion of his discussion to a poetic description of the glory of the great Catholic martyrs. Newman himself was a morbidly sensitive man who seems to have thrived on feelings of persecution; his sense of being a lonely, misunderstood martyr may have sustained him through his darkest periods. He probably believed that his fellow Catholics would also thrive on feelings of persecution. But though I admire many martyrs,[2] I am not anxious to be one, and I strongly suspect that most Roman Catholics share my disinclination.

III. The Narrowness of Newman's Perspective

Newman was in many ways ahead of his time, and it is easy to see why he has been perceived by many as one of the guiding spirits behind the reforms of Vatican II. Still, he was a Victorian thinker who would have been puzzled and troubled by many recent theological and social developments. In his insistence on the importance of an educated Catholic laity and of consulting the laity in matters of doctrine, and in other areas as well, he showed himself to be a progressive mind in certain important ways. But I have grave doubts about many recent attempts to depict Newman as a major forerunner of contemporary ecumenical movements.

Newman seems to have had rather little interest in promoting constructive contacts between Catholics and members of other religious minorities. His principal interest in English dissenters and non-Christians was as potential proselytes, people who could be brought into the True Fold. He despised most defenders of

Protestantism at least as much as they despised him, and he was prepared to write them off without a conciliatory word. All too common in his writings are such statements as, "Methodism is ridiculous, so is Puritanism" (*Prepos.*, sec. 5). And though some of his more zealous admirers have scoffed at the charge, he was a theological anti-Semite who portrayed the Jews as a cursed people.[3] (He almost surely had a bad influence in this regard on such characters as Belloc). Newman's main ecumenical activities were those in which he attempted to bridge the gap between Catholicism and Anglicanism, but even in this area he was not much of a conciliator. In his early Anglican period, when he was trying to conceive of the Anglican church as representing a *via media*, he was hostile to the Church of Rome. In later years, his principal objective in the ecumenical sphere was not simply to make peace between Anglicans and Catholics but to bring Anglicans into the Catholic Church. It can be argued that it was in the spirit of ecumenism that Newman argued for reforms in the Catholic Church that would make it more attractive to Anglicans and other Christians. But the ecumenical spirit does not coalesce easily with the more traditional proselytizing spirit.

In the discussion that we have been considering, Newman reminds his audience that he is speaking "almost in a worldly way; I do not speak to you of Christian charity, lest I should adopt a tone too high for the occasion" (*Prepos.*, sec. 5). While he observes that it is moral as well as prudent to have virtuous dispositions, and to be noble and straightforward in one's dealings with Protestants, his discussion is not really concerned with the subject of the duties of Catholics toward Protestants, but rather with the subject of the duties of Catholics toward the Protestant view of Catholics and the Catholic Church. It is primarily concerned, as we have seen, with a question of prudence: how to respond to anti-Catholic prejudice. Only in the fifth of his sixth prescriptions does Newman deal directly with the subject of the Catholic's moral duties to his non-Catholic neighbors. Because he has emphasized prudential rather than moral considerations, Newman has largely ignored two relevant subjects. He does not speak at any length about the duties of

Catholics to enlightened, tolerant Protestants and their view; he prefers to suggest that there are too few enlightened Protestants to merit special consideration. And he does not discuss the duties of English Catholics and other Catholics to Protestants and other non-Catholics outside of England. It could, of course, be argued that this subject is not relevant to Newman's theme. Anti-Catholicism in England, however, was at least partly a response to the oppression of Protestants and others in Catholic countries; and surely Victorian Protestants had a right to demand of Newman a broader and more balanced survey, historical and geographical, of Catholic-Protestant relations.

It is worth noting here that Newman was incapable of fully appreciating the value of forms of tolerance and pluralism that most people in the English-speaking world now take for granted. Not long after the restoration of the Catholic hierarchy in England, Pope Pius IX issued the reactionary *Syllabus of Errors* (1864), in which he "reminded" Catholics that in the church's eyes, it is wrong to believe, among other things, that, "The Church ought to be separated from the State, and the State from the Church." Newman was not very enthusiastic about some of the items on Pius's list of "errors," but he did try hard to be an obedient Catholic, and even if he had a personal propensity to look favorably on now fashionable forms of tolerance and pluralism—which, for the most part, he did not—he would not have defended them. So again Newman was at a disadvantage in working out his defensive system, for he could not attack such institutions as that of an "established" church, all real and serious obstacles to the liberty of religious minorities.

IV. The Value of Newman's Prescription

I have indicated what I take to be the main weaknesses of Newman's strategy, but I have not recommended a specific alternative, and indeed I have no intention of doing so. Religious bigotry is a complex phenomenon that has many sources, takes numerous forms, and has various dimensions (psychological, sociological, epistemological, theological, and so forth). I find it hard to believe that there is any concrete situation in which the appropriate response to religious prejudice is, as Newman claims, "obvious and simple" (*Prepos.*, secs. 1–2). But controversialists rush in where academic philosophers fear to tread, and we sometimes have good reason to be thankful that they do. People in trouble often need simple, concrete advice, and since philosophers and social scientists cannot or will not provide it, those who do can perform a vital service. Analyses like Newman's may be simplistic, but they are often functional and sometimes irreplaceable.

Neither Newman nor the contemporary historian should be perceived as an infallible authority on the situation of English Catholics in 1851. What Newman lacked in objectivity, the contemporary historian lacks in proximity and involvement. No one can know for sure whether most Catholics living in Birmingham in 1851 would have been better or worse off for following all of Newman's recommendations. Newman did not know, either; his theorizing was highly speculative. He did not claim that his advice is of value to all victims of anti-Catholic prejudice; his aims were rather more limited, and it is I who have suggested that his ideas on countering religious prejudice may have a broad and continuing relevance. Also, I cannot assert with complete confidence that the weaknesses of Newman's strategy necessarily—in any particular situation or in all conceivable situations—outweigh its strengths. Over the centuries, people of different faiths have adopted numerous strategies for countering religious prejudice; they have even adopted the "strategy" of having no strategy. Some responses to religious prejudice have had disastrous consequences; others have simply been ineffective; still others have only been temporarily effective. Sometimes there comes a point when a once effective defensive strategy has outlived its usefulness. Some strategies have worked here but not there. Much can be said for an eclectic strategy; one like Newman's is systematic but one-dimensional. In any case, no amount of theorizing is an adequate substitute for experimentation, though we obviously need to have theories *with which* to experiment. Certainly our primary needs in this area are educational theories and educational experiments, for ultimately it is on the battleground of education that the war against prejudice is won or lost.

John Henry Newman has presented us with interesting, provocative proposals on how to respond to at least a certain kind of religious prejudice. He has thus provided our generation with some theories with which to experiment. Prejudice against Catholics is still much alive in many quarters, and I suspect that it will be with us for many years to come. Catholics at least periodically need to think about what they are going to do about it. Most Catholics also need to work harder at empathizing with non-Catholic victims of religious prejudice, and particularly those who have suffered disabilities as a result of Catholic intolerance. In reflecting on Newman's proposals, we not only gain a useful insight into the complex mind of one of the most influential of religious thinkers, but we gain a deeper understanding of the complexity of a constellation of disconcertingly persistent personal and social problems.

Notes

1. John Henry Newman, "Duties of Catholics Towards the Protestant View," in *Lectures on the Present Position of Catholics in England* (1870 [1851]).

2. See Jay Newman, "The Motivation of Martyrs: A Philosophical Perspective," *The Thomist* 35 (1971): 581–600.

3. See especially John Henry Newman, *An Essay in Aid of a Grammar of Assent* (1870), ch. 10, sec. 2, pt. 6.

Part III

Personal Belief

10
Enlargement of Mind and Religious Judgment in *Loss and Gain*
Michael Martin

At the beginning of Chapter III of *Loss and Gain* Newman wrote concerning the religious standing of the novel's protagonist, Charles Reding, and of Reding's antagonist, William Sheffield, that "Neither of the friends had what are called *views* in religion" by which Newman meant that "neither of them . . . had placed their religion on an intellectual basis." Those who possessed no "views" were incapable of ordering isolated facts and perceptions into a meaningful whole. They could not understand the "connexion of fact with fact, . . . the bearing of fact upon truth,;" they could not "locate" any fact because they possessed "no system." Those who possessed no "views" were utterly incapable of either logical argument or sound judgment for their minds possessed "no one centre . . . (from) . . . their judgment of men and things proceeds." Indeed, by stating that Reding and Sheffield had no "views," Newman indicated that their thought could not at this point possess consistency—by which Newman clearly meant both logical consistency and, more importantly, "constancy." Religiously, they could belong to various "parties" without really believing in the principles which underlay them (*LG*, 14–16).[1]

The story in *Loss and Gain* of Charles Reding's movement from an inherited, previously unquestioned Episcopalianism to an intellectually founded, secure Roman Catholicism was the biography of his acquiring "views," his maturing intellectually to the point where he could place his religion "on an intellectual basis." I do not mean that Reding would "replace" his "faith" with philosophic doctrine—not even in the sense of neo-scholastic theology. His "faith" or "belief" in the "dogmatic principle" stands as a constant throughout the story. The novel chronicles the "enlargement" of Reding's intellect which finally allowed him to judge the intellectually necessary consequences of that belief.

A vexing tension in *The Idea of a University* arose from Newman's distinction between "*teaching* universal *knowledge*" and undertaking any "religious training." Newman correctly perceived an educational dilemma resulting from its institutional situation: how to build a university under the auspices of Catholic episcopal authorities which would not have its mission as a university compromised by its relationship to those authorities. By insisting a university properly defined would teach "universal knowledge," Newman sought to justify admitting theology into the curriculum. Still, while the study of religion was necessary to the university's curriculum, admitting theology as a subject did not mean undertaking religious training: "If (the university's) object were . . . religious training," Newman wrote, "I do not see how it can be the seat of literature and science" (*Idea*, 5).[2] In a phrase, Newman's university would remain, in substance, non-catechetical. But how, then, could a university education which was not "training in religion" benefit the "spiritual welfare" of its students and thereby increase their "religious usefulness and influence" (*Idea*, 6–7). That is, how could knowledge and reason minister to faith. To answer this question, we need to look inside Newman's curriculum.

In his "Preface," Newman announced that his university program should attempt to aid young students to acquire "the steadfastness, the comprehensiveness and versatility of intellect, the command over (their) powers, the instinctive just estimate of things as they pass before (them)." This, he declared, constituted "real cultivation of the mind." Young boys "talk at random," were "flippant," were "what is emphatically called *young*;" intellectually, "they are merely dazzled by phenomena, instead of perceiving things as they are." If, however, the "intellect has once been properly trained and formed," it will come to posses a "connected view or grasp of things" (*Idea*, 10–11).

"The first step in intellectual training (was then) to impress upon a boy's mind the idea of science, method, order, principle and system." The object being to provide the "boy" with "the conception of development and arrangement around a common centre." "Method" was the key: if the boy gained the "habit of method" he would gradually be initiated into the largest and truest philosophical views. By introducing the boy to method, the educator also inoculated him against one of the "chief evils of the day," becoming the modern "intellectual man" who was "full of *views* on all matters" (*Idea*, 12–13). To be "full of views," is here equated with "viewiness," or a "spurious philosophism." Here, I want to note a distinction between possessing "the largest and truest philosophical views" deemed as the positive result of method and "being full of views" deemed a chief evil of the day.

Newman provided a means for distinguishing between "philosophical" and lesser views in his extended discussion of the place of theology in the institution of "universal knowledge." Rhetorically, Newman avoids addressing—at this point—the role of religion in education and reduces the question to a tautology: can the university, defined as the place for teaching "universal knowledge," exclude any branch of knowledge without self contradiction? That is, how does it effect the other sciences and knowledge as a whole, when you exclude theology from the university?

Newman begins his Fourth Discourse with the elevated claim that "Truth is the object of knowledge." Truth exists as a "complex fact" comprised of an system of interrelated "particular facts" which "all taken together form one integral subject for contemplation" (*Idea*, 52). The human mind, powerful as it might be, could not take in the whole as a whole or in a single gaze. Rather, it comprehended this "integral subject . . . by degrees and by circuitous advances." Thus time and experience—continued study—were necessary to achieve comprehension of any truth. Knowledge was achieved by approaching this complex fact from various angles, over time. Each attempt

at comprehension yielding only "partial views." Newman
labelled these "partial views" "sciences" (*Idea*, 53–54). They
could not, as such, convey the totality; at least no single science
could comprehend the totality of a complex fact. Individual
sciences, then, were limited and must accept aid from one
another. It was in the whole coordinated assemblage of these
individual sciences that a semblance of complete knowledge of
any object is attained: "Viewed altogether they approximate to a
representation or subjective reflection of the objective truth"
(*Idea*, 54).

Only when the circle of sciences employed in studying an
object or field of knowledge remains unbroken will they have
anything like a true or complete view of the object. And, *ipso
facto*, all remaining subjects suffered if any one—for instance
theology—were excluded from consideration. Indeed, the individual, small case, "sciences" remained, even when their partial
views were compounded, somehow inadequate (*Idea*, 57).
Because they were all on the same level, each independent but
insufficient to the whole and each needing the aid of the others,
no one science among them could rule over any other science or
coordinate the whole. The rule of the sciences, both in their
internal operations and in their external relations to one another,
was the subject of a higher science. Nor did Newman except
theology from this judgment that the sciences were each merely
one amongst equals, in need of supervision, and this was equally
true of natural and revealed theology (*Idea*, 57–58). Not
theology, in any sense, but a "science of science," which
Newman called "Philosophy, in the true sense of the word" ruled
over the partial views provided by the individual studies and
marshalled them into that "larger" "philosophic view" of the
whole.

The order of the sciences—a universality of limited
views—was dictated by the structure of Truth—an interrelated
complex of individual facts—and by the limits of the human
mind—its inability to comprehend the totality in a single glance.
But the nature of the mind seeks to go beyond any one limited
view: "The intellect . . . grasps and forms what need not have

been seen or heard except in its constituent parts." Doing so, the mind "gives them a meaning and invests them with an idea." The mind "philosophizes; for I suppose Science and Philosophy, in their elementary idea, are nothing else but this habit of *viewing*, . . . of throwing (objects) into system" (*Idea*, 74–75). This "habit of *viewing*," inheres in the mind as such. When educated or "cultivated" the mind's "habit of *viewing*" becomes specifically the "philosophical habit," or the habit of uniting all the sciences and subjecting them to the unifying order of a "philosophical view." That is, the object of education was to fit the mind with powers, or sciences, which would enable it to follow its natural disposition to comprehend the world from the "the largest and truest philosophical views."

Newman held that University education should be considered from two aspects: with reference to its subject matter, the various sciences, and with reference to the objects of its teaching activities, the students. He had completed the former with the four Discourses covering the place of Theology within the sciences and his investigation of the necessity of a "Philosophy" or "science of science" which, when attained, engendered the "philosophical habit of mind." Discourse V, "Knowledge Its Own End" began his investigation of university education via its effects on the students. Specifically, "whether and in what sense, its teaching, viewed relatively to the taught, carries the attribute of Utility along with it" (*Idea*, 94).

Newman begins by defining a "Liberal" education as one which engendered a "philosophical habit of mind" (*Idea*, 96). This philosophical habit of mind also provided for a qualitative distinction between the effect of even the whole complex of sciences taken aggragately and the effect of the sciences approached under the guidance of a "science of sciences or Philosophy." Particular studies are the "basis of definite arts" and hence attain "tangible and beneficial" truths in their limited areas. But what, Newman asked rhetorically, was the "fruit" or utility of the "science of sciences," of "Philosophy" as he had defined it? The very "constitution of the human mind" rendered knowledge, "if it be really such, . . . its own reward." This was equally true of that "special Philosophy" which considered the "comprehensive view of truth," which ordered the "relations of science to science," and determined "their mutual bearings and their respective values" (*Idea*, 96–97). This "Knowledge"—capitalized—which is the object of "Liberal" or "Philosophical" education was "something intellectual . . . something which takes a view of things; which reasons upon what it sees . . . which invests it with an idea" (*Idea*, 104–5). In fact, to obtain this "Liberal Knowledge" was to answer the need of our very nature and support our natural drive to self perfection (*Idea*, 97–98)—true "cultivation of the mind" and a "formation of character" (*Idea*, 105). Science as the study of knowledge was certainly meritorious as the acquisition of the substance, the facts as we might say, about the world. Nevertheless, the end of education was not limited to this acquisition. Knowing the whole encyclopedia of knowledge derived from the study of all the sciences would not constitute being "educated" in the sense Newman means by "Liberal Education" as the "cultivation of the mind." The growth of powers not the acquisition of knowledge, constituted the proper object of Liberal Education as "cultivation of the mind": "it educates the mind to reason well in all matters, to reach out towards truth, and to grasp it" (*Idea*, 114). What Newman seeks from Liberal Education, then, was a "state of mind": the power of judgment.

Newman deals with this issue by investigating "Knowledge viewed in Relation to Learning" where learning designates principles of judgment. Here he expanded on his earlier characterization of the school boy stating :"He has opinions, religious, political, and literary," as a boy he is "very positive in them," but "he gets them from his school fellows or his masters or his parents." Hence, while he may be "observant, sharp, ready, retentive; he is almost passive in the acquisition of knowledge" (*Idea*, 115–16). However, when he passes from school days to the university a change must occur—which the public frequently does not comprehend. The school boy, taking in both knowledge and opinion from those around him, must cease to be passive, he must move from reception of knowledge to "enlargement" of the mind.

> The enlargement . . . is the action of a formative power, reducing to order and meaning the matter of our acquirements; . . . It is not the mere addition to our knowledge . . . the movement onwards, of (a) mental centre . . . a truly great intellect . . . takes a connected view of old and new, past and present, far and near, . . . without which there is no whole, and no centre. It possesses . . . knowledge not merely considered as acquirement, but as philosophy. (*Idea*, 120–21)

And this "enlarged" intellect will be one that comes to see the world of knowledge in the same way that Newman seeks to construct his university:

> That only is true enlargement of the mind which is the power of viewing many things at once as one whole, of referring them severally to their true place in the universal system, of understanding their respective values, and determining their mutual dependence. (*Idea*, 122–23)

Education, "Liberal Education," or "true cultivation of the mind" is not "Learning or Acquirement, but rather is Thought or Reason exercised upon Knowledge, or what may be called Philosophy" (*Idea*, 124–25).

Here we have the definition of the "Philosophical View" of things which neither Charles Reding nor his friend Sheffield possessed in religious matters upon the arrival at the university: they did not yet possess the enlargement of intellect which would allow them to correctly judge the relation of fact to fact. They were not yet capable of forming a "view" of the truths of religion: of putting their religion on an intellectual basis.

On their arrival at Oxford Reding and Sheffield possessed quite different personalities. Sheffield, "easily picked up opinions and facts, especially on the controversies of the day," but he did so, as the narrator reveals, "without laying anything very much to heart." Reding's "knowledge" possessed greater merit than Sheffield's "opinions" precisely because Reding "understood more deeply" and "held more practically what he had once received" (*LG*, 4–5). Essentially, Sheffield studied, argued, and played with ideas and opinions; Reding was driven to judge by taking things to heart.

Later, the narrator reveals the meaning of these two characterizations in terms of *viewiness*: Charles was "young," "poetical"—that is he saw things in the best "spring-time beauty" and "gay confusion, which is the principle element of the poetical." Thus though he "understood more deeply," Charles was still too young to "number and sort and measure things," to "gain views," to "advance toward philosophy and truth" by seeing beyond the poetic. While he had, as yet, no view he did have a principle: "He had a great notion of loving everyone—of looking kindly on everyone" (*LG*, 16–17). Sheffield, "fonder of hunting for views, and more in danger of taking up false ones," was never satisfied, "he was critical, impatient to reduce things to system, pushed principles too far, was fond of argument" (*LG*, 18). Reding was too young, open, and inexperienced to possess true "views;" Sheffield possessed not "views" but was "viewy in a bad sense of the word."

While Sheffield was "viewy" he did possess a principle on which he founded his opinions. He declared himself the enemy of all "sham." He saw "shams everywhere" and like the undergraduate in all of us, he wished "there was less fudge and humbug everywhere." His hatred of shams, which led in Sheffield to argumentative viewiness, proved to be precisely the stimulus Reding needed to begin his acquisition of "views." From Sheffield Reding learned that judgment was a necessity: "dogmatic principle." "Contradictions could not both be real . . . . All doctrines could not be equally sound: there was a right and a wrong." More importantly, when Reding began to apply this insistence on judgment to matters of religious belief, he came to several conclusions: people hold "a great many opinions in the world on the most momentous subjects;" they are not all "equally true;" it is our "duty to hold true opinions;" and "it is uncommonly difficult to get hold of them" (*LG*, 58). This necessity of judging the truth and falsity of religious opinions constituted what the narrator termed the *dogmatic principle* which "gradually became an essential element in Charles's religious views." In turn, this necessity of judging caused Reding to ask questions of his teachers which he thought natural points of intellectual curiosity but his instructors found troubling. They were troubling not because the Church of England divines did not have formal answers; the Thirty-Nine Articles were the codification of those answers. Reding's questions were troubling because to his teachers they indicated a dangerous tendency. In a conversation with the tutor Vincent, the tutor admitted that while Reding was not yet a "party man," his "remarks and questions . . . were like a person pushing things *too far*, and wishing to form a *system*." He continued, warning Reding against such "*tendencies*" (*LG*, 73).

The language here is quite interesting: the tutor might warn Reding against these tendencies to "system" as "pushing things *too far*." But *system* was one of the key words Newman used as the goal of liberal education: "The first step in intellectual training is to impress upon a boy's mind the idea of science, method, order, principle and system" (*Idea*, 12). The dogmatic principle was pushing Reding toward a systematic view by questioning and judging. And an Oxford tutor was recommending against what Newman recommended as the first step in education!

Indeed, as a representative of the Anglican Church by virtue of his Oxford status, the tutor Vincent was correct in recommending that Reding avoid this tendency for by the end of the next chapter Reding began to formulate the most dangerous question of all: "What if, after all, the Roman Catholic Church is the true Church?" As a question, this was certainly dangerous ground for an Oxford man. Even more important was the cry which followed the question: "I wish I knew what to believe; no one will tell me what to believe; I am so left to myself" (*LG*, 83). Reding is asking questions, searching for a system, a "view" to provide solutions to religious perplexities. At the same time he seems to be searching for a guide or an authority to answer his questions for him and remove his doubts. But he finds himself alone in his search—at least at this point he finds himself alone. At the beginning of the next academic year, while in transit through London on route to Oxford, Reding received a letter from a friend, Willis by name, declaring that he had converted to Roman Catholicism. In a desperate effort to undo this disaster, Reding goes to visit Willis. A discussion or rather dispute ensues between Reding, Willis, and an older Catholic, Morley, over why Willis had converted. Morley finally asserts that, regardless of their attractions, no Church but the Catholic Church has faith and that Reding himself is without faith. The attack hit Reding's soft spot, it recalled all of the religious controversies at Oxford and his own questions of the previous year. At this point Willis, Reding's friend, pleaded, "Don't stand at the door arguing: but enter the great home of the soul and adore." Reding refused, stating "surely God wills us to be guided by reason; . . . Surely, we ought not act without it" (*LG*, 99–100). Breaking off the dispute, and quite shaken, Reding rehearses the issue:

> He had gone to lecture, and he had been lectured; and he had let out his secret state of mind; no, not let out, he had nothing to let out. He had implied that he was enquiring after religious truth, but every Protestant inquires; he would not be a Protestant if he did not. Of course he was seeking the truth; it was his duty to do so; . . . This was the very difference between Protestants and Catholics; Catholics begin with faith, Protestants with inquiry. (*LG*, 103)

The encounter forced Reding to define the issue he must face: how faith is reconciled with reason.

In the next chapter, Reding reveals what was most attractive to him—and what was, I think, most attractive to Newman himself—about Roman Catholicism. In an argument Sheffield insisted that every Catholic must deny his rational nature placing a "collar round his neck . . . putting the chain into the hands of a priest." Reding responds that Roman Catholicism's provisions for certitude are what most attract him: "I'd give twopence, if someone whom I could trust, would say to me: 'This is true, this is not true.' We should be saved this eternal wrangling" (*LG*, 107).

The argument progresses to examine the basis for Anglican certainty. In discussing a lecture by an Anglican layman on Church governance, Reding and Sheffield hit on the issue of a Church as an institution and a religious faith as a belief system having a "principle," a "creed." Reding did not like the lecture because it had "no principle; that is no fixed, definite religious principle." Sheffield lights on the word claiming that at least one Protestant divine insists that it is the peculiar nature of Christianity that while the New Testament contains no creed "Scripture is full of *principles*" (*LG*, 110–11). If this were so, that Christianity had no creed in scripture, then it could not be a "dogmatic" religion. Reding then pushes the conclusion to its ultimate end: this position would label the Athanasian creed an illegitimate accretion to Christianity.

Newman's use of the word *principles* here can be misleading. The problem can be stated as a question: does scripture contain *a*—in the singular—creed? Principles, here in the plural, corresponds I think to Sheffield's being "viewy" while not possessing a "view." Reding's search for a creed is the search for "method and system" which Newman made so much of in the *Idea of a University*. What seems to be missing in analogy to Newman's *Idea of a University* is the "science of Sciences" or "Philosophy" which viewed all from above and ordered knowledge into a coherent system. Reding then breaks off the discussion claiming fatigue but he does not drop the issue.

At the beginning of the next chapter the narrator describes the effect on Reding's mind of one of his courses. Reding thought the lectures on the Thirty-Nine Articles would be the solution to all his perplexities; it would end all the various debates he had participated in at Oxford. Unfortunately, as the narrator states, "It did not produce this effect on Reding." He began to see that the Articles were "a patchwork . . . and this too on no principle" (*LG*, 112–13). Stopping after a lecture to speak with a tutor, Reding posed a significant question: "Whether,

According to the Articles, divine truth was directly *given* us, or whether we had to *seek* it for ourselves from Scripture." To Charles's mind, Mr. Upton the tutor evaded the issue stating that neither was the case. The Church *"proposed"* saving doctrine and the individual *"proved"* it. For Charles there appeared only one way of proving doctrine: "by *seeking* (in Scripture) for reasons" (*LG*, 113). Then Reding rephrased the question asking "if the Christian Religion allowed of private judgment"? In the narrator's comment, Newman reveals his understanding of the role of reason in the matter of religious belief:

> This was no abstruse question but a very practical one. Had (Reding) asked a Wesleyan or Independent, he would have had an unconditional answer in the affirmative; had he asked a Catholic, he would have been told that we used our private judgment to find the Church, and then the Church superseded it. (*LG*, 114)

Several points can be made from this narratorial comment: First, reason provided the means in any search for the locus of religious authority, then faith required submission to that authority. Or, as Reding put it during a later discussion, "What is faith but the submission of the intellect?" Reding's companion interlocutor in that discussion, his private tutor Carlton, thought this submission "unnatural." Reding disagreed terming this submission *"supernatural"* (*LG*, 178). Second, there is a condemnation here of any temporizing *via media* as avoiding the question of private judgment. The question could not be avoided and the answer would either lie with the Independents or the Catholics. Third, while reason was efficacious, its role was limited.

At this point, I have considered only about one half of the novel—I've no intention of subjecting you to the whole of it—but in the next chapter, Newman's narrator seeks to show how the submission of the reason is not an error. At the same time I think he shows how Catholicism stands to religious opinions as the "science of science" or "Philosophy" does to the limited views of the individual sciences in the university.

Reding had tried to stay aloof from religious controversy "yet his religious views (were) progressing, unknown to himself." This was as the Creator intended; why else would he have given us an intellectual nature? Hence, "If (Reding) was to worship and obey his Creator, intellectual acts, conclusions and judgments, must accompany that worship and obedience." The progress of his "views" may well have been unconscious, so that he knew not "his own belief . . . but then a single discussion"—the language here echoes the *Idea*—"a single discussion . . . would ascertain for him the limits of each opinion as he held it, and the inter-relations of opinion with opinion" (*LG*, 180–81).

In the *Idea*, the relation of science to science had been established as the special realm of the "Science of Sciences" or "Philosophy." In this sense, Reding's religious development is progressing as knowledge did generally within the studies of Newman's university: each science provided a limited "view;" each religious discussion provided an opinion. They remained, however, unsystematic and without constancy. Each true but limited and insecure. In the university knowledge would be ordered by the "Philosophical habit of mind." In religion, opinions would be ordered and made secure by a creed.

> And here we see what is meant when a person says that the Catholic system comes home to his mind, fulfills his ideas of religion, satisfies his sympathies, and the like; and thereupon he becomes a Catholic.

The Catholic creed or idea—not necessarily the church as an institution, but that is another very long essay—brings the searchers mind into order. It does not require the rejection of reason but the faithful subjection of the reason's limited opinions to the "Catholic Creed." Private judgment prepared the believer as the university's limited individual sciences educated the student:

When a man thus constituted within falls under the shadow of
Catholicism without, then that mighty Creed produces an
influence upon him. He sees that it justifies his thoughts,
explains his feelings; he understands that it numbers, corrects,
harmonizes, completes them; . . . then he submits himself to
the Catholic Church, not by process of criticism, but as a pupil
to a teacher. (*LG*, 183–84)

In a sense, we have watched Charles Reding listen to one
theological or liturgical debate after another. The story of his
growth lies beneath this surface. Reding hears these debates
while he "enlarges" his mind. This process finally surfaces when
Reding comes to understand that—as Newman himself
thought—his move from Anglicanism to Roman Catholicism was
not a desperate or irrational act nor the failure of reason but the
intellectually necessary conclusion to be drawn from his faith.
The Catholic Church, or at least the Creed of Catholicism served
in the religious life as "Philosophy" did within the university.
Hence, the Catholic Creed then must be taken up in an analogous
way: "Philosophy" did not mean merely a set of specific logical
conclusions but a habit of mind; Catholicism is not merely a list
of doctrinal positions but, so to speak, a habit of judgment. In
this habit of the informed judgment I think we find the
intellectual ethos of John Henry Newman.

Notes

1. John Henry Newman, *Loss and Gain* (London: James
Burns, 1848; reprinted New York: Garland Press, 1975).
2. John Henry Newman, *Idea of a University*, edited by I. T.
Ker (Oxford: Oxford University Press, 1976).

11
The Letters to Charles Newman as Background to the *Grammar*
Edward J. Enright, O.S.A.

On 18 May, 1863, Newman wrote to Mrs. John Mozley: "It has ever been a hobby of mine (unless it be a truism, not a hobby) that a man's life lies in his letters" (*LD*, XX: 443). In volume two of *Historical Sketches*, he stated that it is in reading correspondence that one can best discover a dead person's "conversation" (*HS*, II, 221). No better example of these thoughts could be found than Newman himself. Newman's argument in the *Grammar of Assent* is in part that one can assent to, have certitude in, concrete matters. The value of the letters as a source of Newman's thought on faith and reason lies precisely in their concreteness, that is, that Newman worked out his ideas—which ideas he stated to Richard Holt Hutton in a letter of February 12, 1870 remained ever the same (*LD*, XXV, 29)—in response to concrete issues raised by his correspondents. Among the earliest illustrations of this fact is the series of letters Newman and his brother Charles Robert exchanged intermittently between 1823 and 1830. Charles might be called the black sheep of the Newman family. After the death of his father in October of 1824, Charles quarreled with the family and gave up Christianity. This took place in the midst of his correspondence with John Henry, who had obtained for him a position with the Bank of England in 1825, which Charles resigned seven years later. Between 1842 and 1845 Charles was at the University of Bonn. He was always supported by the family, both before and after his stay in Germany. In the 1850s, he retired to Tenby, to Alma Cottage, March Road, where he was attended by the landlady, Mrs. Griffith. Charles, who saw no visitors, died in 1882. John Henry paid for his tomb on which he had inscribed "Domine, misericordia tua in seculum, Opera manuum tuarum ne despicias" (*LD*, I, 338).

In an article in the *Dublin Review*, Dr. G. R. Evans writes that Newman wrote a Memorandum in 1874 in which he briefly describes why he believed Charles failed to "make his way in the world." It was Newman's contention that this failure was not due to a "lack of ability," because Charles "was an excellent linguist and had a head for philosophy," nor was it due to a "deficiency of moral sense," because, as Newman put it, Charles "has ever shown himself upright, sensitively honest, generous, open-handed, and affectionate." Newman concluded that it was due to Charles' lack of common sense and a "preposterous pride."[1]

I. The Letters to Charles

The correspondence between Newman and Charles Robert, which began with a letter from Newman on December 12, 1823, was precipitated by a conversation he and Charles had "when walking to Town from Strand the beginning of August last," arguing "from Turnham Green to Knightsbridge" (*LD*, XX, 169). In the letter, Newman explained that since "We find one man of one opinion in religion, another of another," we might "hastily . . . conclude that opinions diametrically opposite to each other may be held without danger to one side or the other in a future state; but contradictions can no more be true in religion," than in science (*LD*, XX, 169). Focusing in on the effect differing opinions would have on the "future state" of one who believes in revelation, he continued the comparison with science, stating that unlike errors in scientific opinions, errors in religious opinions would be attended "with danger to the person who maintains them, he who holdeth not 'the faith', (I am not now determining what that faith is) such a one is said to be incapable of true moral excellence, and so exposed to the displeasure of God."

Therefore, it is necessary, he wrote, "to press upon the conscience . . . that we are playing with edged tools, if instead of endeavoring perseveringly to ascertain what the truth is, we consider the subject carelessly, captiously, or with indifference" (*LD*, XX, 170). It can be said then, that in this letter, Newman expressed his opinion that what one believes has consequences for one's moral state.

Interestingly, the correspondence lapses until early in 1825, when in February, Charles, as Dr. Evans states it, "sent Newman so hot and ill-considered a letter of rejection of the Christian faith that Newman felt it his duty to try to argue him back to sense."[2] Charles wrote to his brother that:

> I am glad to say I have come to a satisfactory conclusion with regard to religion, sooner than could be expected . . . But I (after a great deal of preparatory thought, I acknowledge) have come to a judgment which no doubt will surprise you; for it is entirely against Christianity; which I expected to find synonymous with wisdom and knowledge, but which is far otherwise. I think Mr (Robert) Owen for practical motives to action . . . beats St Paul hollow. (*LD*, I, 212n.1)

Responding on March 3, Newman insisted on the importance and kind of mental disposition for ascertaining truth, be it religious or otherwise. One needs, he wrote, a "calm, equable, candid, philosophical temper." One cannot "be self-willed to decide precipitately to run away with a part for the whole, to form conclusions from very partial inductions, to suffer . . . to be soon excited." Mental "'fidgetiness' and 'itching'" are objections "to the probable correctness of . . . reasonings" (*LD*, I, 213). In the letter of March 24, 1825, Newman took up the point of moral disposition. Rejection of Christianity arises "from a fault of the heart, not of the intellect;" unbelief arises not only from erroneous reasoning, but "from pride or from sensuality" (*LD*, I, 219). Furthermore, Newman implied, if a person is going to judge the reasonableness of religious belief, be it the existence of God or Christianity as a religion, he must already be a believer.

He stated that "the Christian evidences are most convincing, and yet that they are unlikely to convince those who reject them" (*LD*, I, 219). Newman felt that "A dislike of the *contents* of Scripture is at the bottom of unbelief; and since those contents must be rejected by fair means or foul, it is plain that *in order to this* the evidences must in some sort be attacked." For unbelievers, however, this process is but "*an afterthought*," and so they "reverse the legitimate process of reasoning" (*LD*, I, 219). Reiterating this point, he wrote:

> The most powerful arguments for Christianity do not *convince*, only *silence*: for there is at bottom that secret antipathy for the doctrines of Christianity, which is quite out of reach of argument. I do not then assert that the Christian evidences are *overpowering*, but that they are *unanswerable*; nor do I expect so much to show Christianity *true*, as to prove it *rational*; nor to prove infidelity *false*, so much as *irrational*. (*LD*, I, 219)

Prescinding from the presumption of personal belief, which he seemed to indicate is preferable for arguing the reasonableness of Christianity, Newman made a seminal attempt to "demonstrate" this reasonableness by insisting on the distinction between the content of revelation and the evidences for that revelation. Before pursuing this distinction, it is important to note that in the letter of March 3, 1825, to Charles Robert, he stated that "the external evidences are built upon the obvious and general canons by which we judge of the truth or falsehood of everything we hear; not on rules peculiar to religion, or modelled by it . . . the external is founded on purely logical principles" (*LD*, I, 214). He bolstered this opinion in his letter of July 7, 1825, by stating that according to God's ordering of things, a person knows historical facts from probable evidence, and that we become aware of external reality through the senses (*LD*, I, 240). It is precisely historical facts and other external evidences available to the senses that constitute the credentials of revelation. In another vein, he considered the possibility of the intelligibility of revelation to the human mind when he wrote that the idea of revelation implies something, that is, that what is revealed is

> indiscoverable by human reason; nor would it be anything
> strange and revolting to our minds to suppose, that, ignorant
> as we are of the whole plan of Divine Providence, the contents
> of a revelation were such, as when revealed not to fit on to
> what we already knew of his dealings: that is not only
> indescribable; but contrary to what we think we
> know;—though I should contend that this is not the case. (*LD*,
> I, 240–41)

Seemingly, there is a common ground here for believer and unbeliever alike. Newman later went so far as to say in a letter to Charles Robert on August 25, 1825, that he "never denied that his (humankind's) natural feelings and notions are to a certain point correct and to be obeyed" (*LD*, I, 253). Even when he stated in his letter to Charles Robert on April 14, 1825, that what is discovered from the disclosure of revelation may "certainly . . . turn out to be beyond (the) reach" of human experience, he did admit that what is discovered "*may* prove agreeable" (*LD*, I, 225) to that experience.

On the basis of our natural feelings and notions then, it is not being inconsistent to think, Newman had stated in his letter to Charles Robert on August 25, 1825, that "mankind may be right in the feeling of *dependence* on a superior being, a subject on which there *is a general agreement*, and yet wrong in their conceptions of the *object* of that dependence, a point on which there is *a general disagreement*" (*LD*, I, 253). It was precisely because of this disagreement in content that Newman distinguished content and evidences. He repeatedly pointed out the relativity of the content of individual's beliefs, and consequently the necessity of studying the evidences. In his letter to Charles Robert on March 3, 1825, Newman had written that "the internal evidence depends a great deal on moral feeling" (*LD*, I, 214), a feeling which could draw the charge of prejudice. Therefore, he stated in a letter of April 14, 1825, that "it is unfair to form your judgment of a revelation from its moral system"

(*LD*, I, 225).   In the same letter, Newman pointed to another reason for studying the evidences, namely, that anyone who attempts to judge the contents of revelation by his/her own preconceived notions would be acting illogically, because he/she would assume that the same notions were "so demonstratively true, that instead of examining the claims of the revelation he might try it by its contents" (*LD*, I, 225).   He went on to state that someone who would attempt to decide on the truth of the contents of revelation and then use those contents as an objection to the revelation would be guilty of temerity because not only is such a person ignorant of the contents "but liable to be swayed by every variety of passion, temper, and disposition" (*LD*, I, 226).   Again, it is Newman's contention that revelation cannot be judged by its contents because no two people can agree "in their antecedent and self-originating ideas of God and his purposes towards man" (*LD*, I, 226).   In his letter to Charles Robert on July 7, 1825, Newman thought that since humankind is weak, it is incapable of judging the contents (*LD*, I, 240).   Finally, Newman stated in his letter to Charles Robert on July 26, 1825, that it is unfair to judge a revelation by what is revealed because "its credentials are no more contained in the message itself which it purports to bring from heaven, than an ambassador's instructions from his sovereign are his credentials" (*LD*, I, 246–47).

Despite the fact that Newman attempted this defense of the reasonableness of Christianity independent of personal belief by insisting on the distinction between the contents of revelation and the evidences for that revelation—which evidences are to be judged by logical principles—he could never believe in his heart of hearts that a person could come to belief by way of evidences. Instead, he always assumed the existence of a Moral Governor. Furthermore, as he wrote to Charles Robert on April 14, 1825, it is a fundamental doctrine of Christianity that the human mind cannot attain religious truth without a revelation from God, who would also remove the barriers to receiving that revelation (*LD*, I, 228).   Newman counselled Charles that he would find no real knowledge   or   true   peace   without   humble,   sincere,   and

persevering prayer to the Author of Peace, a counsel he repeated
in his letter of July 26.

Except for a letter written on September 26 on biblical
topics, the correspondence between Newman and his brother
Charles Robert ended, until five years later, when, on August 19,
1830, Newman wrote a lengthy letter to Charles on the
reasonableness of belief (*LD*, II, 266–81). There is nothing new
in this letter; in fact Newman frequently quoted passages from
previous letters to reiterate his position. He did, however, write
a "Memorandum on Revelation," dated January 2, 1831, in which
are contained further thoughts on revelation, thoughts which he
had originally intended to include in the letter to his brother on
August 19, 1830, but did not, because he felt that Charles was
not yet ready to deal with them. In the Memorandum, Newman
stated first of all his belief in the universality of revelation.
Revelation can be found unequally in the traditions of the world,
in a variety of ways in the world's religions. A distinction he
made between the Christian Church and every other form of
revelation is that the Christian Church has revelation in a written
form. Implied too is the idea that the Christian Church has
received revelation in its clearest and fullest form, but he also
believed that, even within Christianity, revelation "varies
indefinitely in its degrees—the Romanists have far less of a
revelation than we have" (*LD*, II, 281). Furthermore, all human
beings are given enough revelation to attain heaven and to
change their moral nature for virtue, "For all have a natural
conscience, which at once exhorts them to virtue and by an
instinctive vigor extracts from even the worst religious systems
those better parts and real truths which relate to the being,
providence, and moral governance of God." Therefore, since
"No one is vicious but by his own fault: for conscience and
God's Spirit set him right on his first starting, till he blunts the
one and quenches the other," Newman concluded that Christians
have "peculiar, but not exclusive religious privileges" to know
God and his/her plans toward humankind (*LD*, II, 282).

Newman's "Memorandum on Revelation" also asserted that
the evidence for revelation is not necessarily compelling. No one

is forced to believe, but anyone who seeks the truth is given sufficient evidence to attain the truth. Furthermore, the evidence comes in a variety of forms, for example, "the fact of the present existence of Christianity is an argument from *sense*, in kind the same as if the revelation were written on the sun" (*LD*, II, 282). He also noted that there can be arguments from known facts against revelation, for example, "history against prophecy, or the dictates of conscience against doctrine." However, he warned that since revelation discloses things that are unknown, we cannot judge it by "preconceived notions and arbitrary theories of morals" (*LD*, II, 283).

II. The Letters to Charles and the *Grammar*

The Moral State

A proper moral disposition was so important for Newman that he went so far as to say in a letter to Henry James Coleridge on February 5, 1871, nearly a year after its publication, that the *Grammar* was written "to show that a right moral state of mind germinates or even generates good intellectual principles" (*LD*, XXV, 280). As the letters to Charles have shown, either the moral state affects one's intellectual processes or what one believes affects one's moral state.

It is the former which Newman taught in the eighth chapter of the *Grammar*, when exploring informal inference. There Newman stated that one of the characteristics of the argumentative process which is needed to attain certitude is "the moral state of the parties inquiring or disputing." Then quoting Bishop Butler approvingly, he wrote that these inquiring or disputing parties "must be 'as much in earnest about religion, as about their temporal affairs, capable of being convinced, on real evidence, that there is a God who governs the world, and feel themselves to be of a moral nature and accountable creatures'" (*GA*, 207).[3] If one looks at the letters to Charles in particular, one will find Newman insisting on what Butler states about the

importance of a right moral disposition when approaching matters
of revelation, that otherwise the inquirer could either distort the
evidence or judge revelation by its contents rather than by its
evidence.

Revelation Judged by Its Credentials, Not by Its Contents

Again and again in the letters to his brother Charles the
theme of "revelation" recurs. For Newman, revelation should
never be judged by its contents, but only by its credentials or
evidences. He gave a number of reasons over the course of those
letters for this belief: (1) disagreement in the content of
individual's beliefs; (2) the variety of moral systems based on the
content of revelation; (3) the attempt to judge the contents of
revelation by pre-conceived notions; (4) lack of agreement
between people "in their antecedent and self-originating ideas of
God and his purposes toward man" (*LD*, I, 226);[4] (5) the
weaknesses of humankind, that is, that revelation is itself
required for belief, because the human mind cannot relate to the
divine without it; (6) the absence of credentials in the contents of
revelation. Newman's concern in insisting on the distinction
between revelation's contents and credentials seems to have been
the desire to find a common ground by which all persons of good
will would be able to communicate about revelation.

In the introduction to Chapter Ten of the *Grammar*, Newman
referred to "Gospel Revelation," making the distinction between
its divinity and the evidence for that divinity. This seems to be
a concrete expression of the distinction between the contents and
evidences of revelation he had made in the letters to Charles. He
then proceeded to say why he had made this distinction, that is,
that "a revelation might have been really given, yet given without
credentials. Our supreme Master might have imparted to us
truths which nature cannot teach us, without telling us He had
imparted them." He gave the example of what he called
"heathen countries" in which God's revelation can be found, but
the source of which the people of those nations are unaware. He
contrasted this type of revelation with that of the Christian, which

he described as "Revelatio revelata," "a definite message from God to man distinctly conveyed by His chosen instruments, and to be received as such a message" (*GA*, 249). Consequently, he wrote in the next paragraph, "the exhibition of credentials, that is, of evidence, that it is what it professes to be, is essential to Christianity, as it comes to us" (*GA*, 250).

Revelation Natural to the Human Mind

In the letters to Charles, Newman made two other important points, which overlap each other. He pointed out that the external evidences for revelation "are built upon the obvious and general canons by which we judge of the truth or falsehood of everything we hear; not on rules peculiar to religion, or modelled by it . . . the external is founded on purely logical principles" (*LD*, I, 214).[5] In another letter to Charles Robert on July 7, 1825, he considered the possibility of the intelligibility of revelation to the human mind, stating that while revelation is "indiscoverable by human reason," and therefore might not "fit on to what we already knew of his (God's) dealings" (*LD*, I, 241), maybe even contrary to what we think we know, he would not contend that this is the case. Revelation and the human intellect are not necessarily incompatible.

In the "Memorandum on Revelation" of January 2, 1831, Newman stated his belief in the universality of revelation. Revelation can be found unequally in the traditions of the world, in a variety of ways in the world's religions. Furthermore, since all human beings are given enough revelation for the attainment of conversion and eternal life, therefore Newman concluded that Christians have "peculiar, but not exclusive religious principles" (*LD*, II, 282) to know God and his/her plans toward humankind.

In the *Grammar* the idea of revelation being natural to the human mind is present, but couched in the format of revealed religion resting on natural religion, which is itself a universal phenomenon. Two brief quotes from the *Grammar* can represent Newman's continued belief in the naturalness of revelation to the human mind. He noted "how congenial the notion of a revelation is to the human mind, so that the expectation of it may truly be considered an integral part of Natural Religion" (*GA*, 260–61). When discussing revealed religion, he asked "Is it not wise to argue from what we actually know to what we do not know?" (*GA*, 271).

When discussing the universality of revelation in the "Memorandum on Revelation" (January 2, 1831) Newman had stated that all human beings have a natural conscience, "which at once exhorts them to virtue and by an instinctive vigor extracts from even the worst religious systems those better parts and real truths which relate to the being, providence, and moral governance of God" (*LD*, II, 282). While Newman devoted attention to the subject of conscience in Chapter Four of the *Grammar*, when discussing the notional assent called "Presumption," and in a major section of the fifth chapter in the same work, it is when discussing natural religion in the tenth chapter that his ideas on conscience are most pertinent to the subject of revelation. What was stated in the "Memorandum on Revelation" on conscience is certainly implied here in the *Grammar* when he stated that "Conscience is nearer to me than any other means of knowledge," that is, knowledge of God. "Our great internal teacher of religion is . . . our conscience." Furthermore, conscience "provides for the mind a real image of Him . . . it gives us a rule of right and wrong, as being His rule, and a code of moral duties" (*GA*, 251).

Revelation Is Not Necessarily Compelling

Another belief Newman expressed in the "Memorandum on Revelation" was that the evidence for revelation is not necessarily compelling. No one is forced to believe, but anyone who seeks the truth is given sufficient evidence to attain the truth (*LD*, II, 282). In the tenth chapter of the *Grammar*, Newman wrote that the truth of Christian revelation "rests upon grounds intrinsically and objectively and abstractedly demonstrative, but it does not follow from this that the arguments producible in its favor are unanswerable and irresistible." A few lines later he wrote that "The fact of revelation is in itself demonstrably true, but it is not therefore true irresistibly; else, how comes it to be resisted?" (*GA*, 264).

Conclusion

In conclusion, it can be said without hesitation, that the consistency in Newman's teaching on the moral state, revelation, and conscience in the letters to his brother Charles Robert and the "Memorandum on Revelation" one the one hand, and the *Grammar of Assent* on the other, vindicated his belief, expressed in a letter to Richard Holt Hutton on February 13, 1870, that his thought on such subjects remained basically the same over the course of his career (*LD*, XXV, 29), and therefore vindicates my contention that Newman's correspondence, and in the particular case of the correspondence with Charles and the "Memorandum," constitutes significant historical background to the *Grammar*.

Notes

1. G. R. Evans, "Newman's Letters to Charles," *The Downside Review* 100 (1982): 92.

2. Evans, "Newman's Letters to Charles," 92.

3. John Henry Newman, *An Essay in Aid of a Grammar of Assent*, ed. I. T. Ker (Oxford: Clarendon Press, 1985).

4. April 14, 1825, Newman to Charles Robert Newman.

5. March 3, 1825 (see July 7, 1825), Newman to Charles Robert Newman.

12
The Lonergan Connection with Newman's *Grammar*
Carla Mae Streeter, O.P.

It is an awesome moment in theological study to come upon the relationship between two intellectual giants. This essay will be concerned with such a connection, that between John Henry Newman, convert and cardinal, and Bernard J. F. Lonergan, cradle Catholic and Canadian Jesuit. Newman died in 1890, and Lonergan almost a century later, in 1984. Both had similar concerns: to offer the world an option to the secular liberalism, relativism, and scientism that had no place for religious mystery. The direction these two great minds took to open up this option was to meet the opposition on its own ground, the forum of the mind. Both begin phenomenologically, seeking to chart the movement of the mind toward certainty. Both were committed men of faith, Catholics, who were determined to include in their charting the reality and value of religious belief for modern day culture.

This brief essay will begin with Newman, and specifically the foundation he lays in *The Grammar of Assent*.[1] The essay will consider the origin of the *Grammar*, the purpose Newman had in writing it, and the point that he wants to make. We will then turn to a consideration of Lonergan, and how he builds and expands on the foundation Newman has laid. Finally we will ask what this might imply for those who are doing theology in a North American context at the brink of the twenty-first century.

I. The Newman Foundation

The *Grammar* appears to have been written in response to a public accusation that Newman accepted as true. Editor Richard Simpson, in the December 1858 issue of "The Rambler," accuses Newman of writing "colossal fragments" while never producing a "finished edifice."[2] Newman had just returned from his term as first rector of the Catholic University of Dublin. It was at Dublin that he had delivered the series that eventually became the contents for *The Idea of a University*. A month after Simpson's accusation appeared, Newman began work on a writing he called "Discursive Enquiries on Metaphysical Subjects." By September of 1859, as the archives of Birmingham reveal, he began work on a section called "Formation of Mind." On January 15 of 1860 he received the letter from his friend, William Froude, considered by many to be the most immediate cause of the writing of the *Grammar*. William Froude wrote that his growing appreciation of the rigorous standards of scientific investigation was moving him further and further into skepticism and agnosticism.[3] The conviction was growing in Newman that the time was growing short for producing a coherent defense of faith against the liberalist zeitgeist. Catholic intellectuals were under siege.

Newman's article, "On Consulting the Faithful in matters of Doctrine," appeared in *The Rambler* in July of 1859. It caused a stir, making his orthodoxy suspect in the eyes of the Hierarchy. He abandoned his "Discursive Enquiries" project as adding fuel to the fire of the growing tension, and began a simple collection of theologico-philosophical reflections. He worked away at response after response to Froude's dilemma. By 1866 he formulated a writing plan for the *Grammar*, and in 1870 he completed it.

In a note added to the *Grammar* in 1880, Newman gives us the clear purpose of the work. He wrote to describe the *"Organum Investigandi,"* the process of investigation, keeping in mind religious and theological truth as part of the quest of the investigator. This argumentative work "in defense of my creed," is intended to take on any who would accuse Newman of a blind pietism (*GA*, 382f.).

The point Newman drives home in this final work is that the process of the mind is a circling and spiralling movement, precisely what Newman himself experienced in his own conversion, and what was happening as he had set out to gather his "colossal fragments" into a "finished edifice." There are elements to this *Novum Organum Investigandi*. There are assumptions and first principles, premises which enter in, ethico-personal dispositions, and a mode of arranging and considering the matter for debate.

The method to be followed was phenomenological. It does not merely state former conclusions, but is concerned with the life and structure of our cognitional and ethical nature as it unfolds in its own operations. Newman will search for this recurring pattern in his own consciousness, and then ask his readers to verify for themselves the truth of the assertions he has made. This self-appropriation completed, it remains but for one to apply this method theologically.[4]

The unique discovery of Newman in this process is what he names the "Illative Sense." It is the mind's power to judge or conclude in the concrete, not in the abstract (*GA*, 271, 276). Norris describes it in this way:

> According to logic, which is the formal exhibition of all demonstrative science, the only certain conclusions are deductions from self-evident principles: theories, hypotheses and opinions may have any degree of probability, but they can never be certainties, for absolute verification is not possible. For Newman, however, the illative sense is just such an absolute verification, because it is able to establish the focal point of an otherwise inconclusive evidence, meeting a question in the spirit, though not in the letter, of rationality. It concludes a process, too complex for easy and complete articulation, too elusive and minute for adequate analysis, and too rich in its data for restricted methods.[5]

Newman creates his own terms to explain what he means. Formal Inference for the liberal thinker is the only way to certainty. For Newman, inference is the conditional acceptance of a proposition. Assent, in contrast, is the unconditional acceptance of a proposition: "The object of Assent is a truth, the object of Inference is the truth-like" (*GA*, 209). For Newman, acts of inference are both the antecedents of assent before assenting, and its usual concomitant after assenting.[6]

Assent does not have the reasoning character possessed by inference, but the two are compatible. Simple assent is an *unconscious* act of unconditional acceptance, while complex or reflex assent for Newman is a *conscious* and deliberate act of unconditional acceptance. Certitude as a mental state is a complex assent to a notional or imaginative proposition.[7] The key to what Newman is trying to clarify in the *Grammar* is the careful distinction between assent and inference.[8]

Although distinct in his approach, Newman is in harmony with the intellectual emphasis of Aquinas. The mind is not a pawn, but a source of its own results. It is Newman's genius to have begun to chart its operations. It will be the task of another genius, almost a century later, who will build on that foundation.

II. The Lonergan Edifice

Bernard J. Lonergan was born in Buckingham in the province of Quebec, Canada, in 1904. He died at the Jesuit infirmary at Pickering, east of the city of Toronto, in 1984 just a few weeks short of his eightieth birthday. Lonergan is often indiscriminately classified with Transcendental Thomists. His own comment on this can be found in *Method in Theology*:

> In his book, *The Transcendental Method*, New York: Herder and Herder, 1968, Otto Muck works out a generalized notion of transcendental method by determining the common features in the work of those that employ the method. While I have no objection to this procedure, I do not consider it very pertinent

to an understanding of my own intentions. I conceive method concretely. I conceive it, not in terms of principles and rules, but as a normative pattern of operations with cumulative and progressive results. I distinguish the methods appropriate to particular fields and, on the other hand, their common core and ground, which I name transcendental method. Here, the word, transcendental, is employed in a sense analogous to Scholastic usage, for it is opposed to the categorial (or predicamental). But my actual procedure also is transcendental in the Kantian sense, inasmuch as it brings to light the conditions of the possibility of knowing an object in so far as that knowledge is *a priori*.[9]

An air of mystery, almost a mystique surrounds Bernard Lonergan. Serious readers who begin a tentative exploration into Lonergan's thought by reading the first five chapters of *Insight* often go no further. While it is true that Lonergan is about a distinct project and cannot easily be categorized with a specific type of Thomist approach, he can be quite accessible to students who have some acquaintance with Newman's thought. In Lonergan's own words it serves us well to begin to gather an idea of the connection.

Philosophic reflection has to sort out the two manners (of knowing), to overcome regressive tendencies to childish feelings and ways, and to achieve the analytic task of disentangling the many components in human knowing and the different strands in its objectivity. A list of the different ways one can go wrong will provide, I believe, a thumbnail sketch of most of the main philosophical systems. . . . there is the question whether my prior allegiance to Thomism did not predetermine the results I reached. Now it is true that I spent a great deal of time in the study of St. Thomas and that I know I owe a great deal to him. I just add, however, that my interest in Aquinas came late. As a student in . . . philosophy . . . in the twenties I . . . went through the main parts of Newman's *Grammar of Assent* six times. . . . Only later in that decade, when studying theology, did I discover the point to the real distinction (in knowing) by concluding the *unicum esse* from the Incarnation and by relating Aquinas' notion of *esse* to Augustine's of *veritas*. Finally, it was in the forties that I began to study Aquinas on cognitional theory, and as soon as the *Verbum* articles were completed (*Theological Studies*, 1946–49), I began to write *Insight*.[10]

This sketch of his own intellectual development is followed by other references to his own development in relation to that early acquaintance with Newman:

Newman's remark that ten thousand difficulties do not make a doubt has served me in good stead. It encouraged me to look difficulties squarely in the eye, while not letting them interfere with my vocation or my faith. His illative sense later became my reflective act of understanding.[11]

Chapters nine, ten, and eleven (of *Insight*) have to do with judgment. Chapter nine endeavors to say what we mean by judgment. Chapter ten investigates the immediate ground of judgment and finds it in a grasp of the virtually unconditioned, a view that was preceded in my thinking by some acquaintance with Newman's illative sense.[12]

One can gain a helpful grasp of the "edifice" Lonergan builds in *Insight* with an initial reading of "Insight Revisited" in *A Second Collection*.[13] Such a reading gives one the sense that what Newman began has been carried to an intricate analysis.

It was Lonergan's intent to write *Insight* as the first of a two volume project. The second volume was to be *Method in Theology*, rounding out the study to include the role of religion and faith in a thorough understanding of what knowing is. The density of *Insight* required Lonergan to wait four years until a publisher was found for his manuscript in 1957. *Insight* had been finished in 1953. With its completion Lonergan was assigned to the Gregorianum in Rome to teach, and a ten year hold was put on the completion of the second volume. The wait was providential. During his Roman period Lonergan wrestled with the doctrines of the Trinity and the Incarnation, producing significant Latin works that now in translation are only beginning to be known. Most importantly, Lonergan wrestled with existentialism and with an international community of students. These two elements served to bring an exposure that would otherwise be missing from *Method in Theology* which appeared in book form in 1970 after numerous lectures on its contents.

One who reads *Insight* without knowing that *Method* is its completion does not know the complete Lonergan, for his purpose, like Newman's, is apologetic. That purpose is to meet those who would dispense with faith and religious love on their own terms: the operations of the mind as it seeks truth.

As with Newman, the beginning is phenomcnological. The attention is to what we do by nature to know. The sciences, both natural and human, know what it means to begin with data. Lonergan will challenge them to widen their horizon on this data, including not only the data of sense, but the data of consciousness. The data of consciousness needs to be observed, it needs to be objectified, charted. The results will be a cognitional theory based on objectifying the operations of the intelligence as it moves toward judgment, toward knowing. As this process is noted, its pattern is reaffirmed again and again. An epistemology becomes possible for the first time based on empirical data, the data of consciousness. It becomes possible to ask why *this* is knowing, and nothing else is. It will be this data, the data of consciousness of the human operator, that becomes the locus for the in-breaking of grace and the theological life of faith, hope, and charity that give evidence of its presence.

Newman had envisioned an "*Organon Investigandi*."[14] He had laid its foundations. But he also realized that he had but begun this momentous project.

> You have truly said that we need a *Novum Organum* for theology—and I shall be truly glad if I shall be found to have made any suggestions which will aid the formation of such a calculus—but it must be the strong conception and the one work of a great genius, not the obiter attempt of a person like myself, who has already attempted many things, and is at the end of his days. (*LD*, XXV, 56–57)[15]

The edifice that Lonergan builds on Newman's remarkable foundation is an empirical account of Aquinas' intelligence in act. Beginning with the phantasm that arises out of the data of sense or consciousness, Lonergan traces the dynamism of the human intelligence. The dynamism manifests itself in distinct questioning. Questions for inquiry leads to insight or the pivotal linking of elements of imagery. The linking enables a concept to form. Questions for reflection move the mind into a judgment of the truth of the insight, an expansion of Newman's illative sense. Questions of value move the human agent into a judgment of value which triggers choice.

It is helpful here to recall that Lonergan's thesis dealt with operative and cooperative grace in Thomas Aquinas. In terms of cognition this theological focus becomes the backdrop for Lonergan's use of the expression "vector." The upward vector becomes the mind moving in its step by step pattern from the simple experiential awareness of data through insight, conceptualization, to judgment, and finally choice. The downward vector is the dynamic of being grasped by religious love, which manifests itself first in a judgment of value, a commitment, and then proceeds to seek the understanding of what one knows in faith. This downward movement or healing vector is a functional explanation of what we have known as sanctifying grace. The healing is *for* the creative movement of the mind freed for its intended pattern of operation. Much remains to be done on an exploration of how Newman's stress on the imagination is critical in the whole process of understanding. Lonergan deals with it only in a beginning way in chapter XVII of *Insight*.[16]

The implications for the human agent as a believer need to be drawn out. If Lonergan's analysis is correct, then we have for the first time the grounding of the grace dynamic in human consciousness and in human knowing. We have the beginnings of an explanation, not merely a description, of the dynamic of grace as it functions in total respect of the human intelligence, yet providing it a certainty it experiences but does not understand.

III. Implications for Theology

Newman's concern, the undermining of faith by a growing secular world view, has become a lived reality for our generation. Relativism, and the abandonment of the search for Truth among many partial truths, is rampant on our university campuses. Young people have little or no light to find their way out of the maze. Little, that is, unless someone opens to them the marvelous operations of their own minds. For this indeed is the *organon*, and knowing its pattern opens to one the *Novum Organum Investigandi* that Newman had the vision to foresee would be needed.

One only needs to pick up a best seller such as Alan Bloom's *The Closing of the American Mind*[17] to explore the impact of this rudderless intellectualism in the American context. It manifests itself in ethical areas, in power economics and authority questions, and in much vacuous theology.

The contribution of these two giants provides a light in this intellectual darkness. This is not because they provide answers, but because they have given us a clarity on that which seeks the answers, our own intelligences, and the definite place both reason and faith have in that quest. Without sound cognitional theory the direction pointed by such consciousness philosophers as Gadamer, Polanyi, and Voeglin becomes only a vision with no means of attainment except desire. Newman and Lonergan are convinced that desire is destined to be realized, and have charted the means.

As we move toward the turn of the century, we carry with us a development in the natural and human sciences that has never been so developed in our human history. There is at the same time an unprecedented hunger for the ultimate Reality toward which each of the sciences with its specific content focus converges. This provides a climate for the dialogue of theology with the natural and human sciences unlike any so far in our history. The question becomes, where will theology enter the dialogue? Will it be able to speak the empirical language of the sciences and recognizing that starting place lead the partners to a sound explanation of the divine working *within* the material world? What is the significance of sound cognitional theory in the doing of sound theology? Perhaps for the first time we have an empirical anthropological base for theology to open up the ultimate concerns of the sciences. This could mean a *functional* reclaiming of theology as completion of the sciences.

These are the challenges that lie before us as philosophers, and as theologians. We have need of Aquinas in a new key. We have need to stand on the shoulders of a Newman, and we have need to begin the intellectual sweat-work that Lonergan suggests will be our only solution to the problem of the total decline of culture. His solution is one that builds on Newman's concern. We have need, in Lonergan's words, of "a divinely sponsored collaborative solution" that provides us for the first time with explanatory categories in consciousness for the dynamism of faith, hope, and religious love as they enable the human to function in the renewal of culture.[18] This is the task of the *Novum Organum Investigandi* in theology.

What lies ahead is the building of a world community. This community will need a new economic world order. Theology has need of new categories to deal with the activity of God in religious traditions unknown to most theologians. Culture, regarded for the first time in history in its rich empirical diversity will move into rudderless decline without the guiding hand of sensitive intelligence.

In the truest sense, the intellectual vision of John Henry Newman is a summons to the human community. We have within us the means for our own progress. It is both sobering and electrifying to realize that the divine is once again waiting upon a "Let it be done."

Notes

1. John Henry Newman, *An Essay in Aid of A Grammar of Assent*, ed. Nicholas Lash (Notre Dame, IN: University of Notre

Dame Press, 1979).

2. Thomas J. Norris, *Newman and His Theological Method: A Guide for the Theologian Today* (Leider, Netherlands: E. J. Drill, 1977), 23.

3. Norris, *Newman and His Theological Method*, 24.

4. Norris, *Newman and His Theological Method*, 27–28.

5. Norris, *Newman and His Theological Method*, 42–43.

6. George W. Rutler, "Newman on Assent to Religious Belief," in, George W. Rutler, *Christ and Reason: An Introduction to Ideas from Kant to Tyrrell* (Front Royal, VA: Christendom Press, 1990), 59 92, at 82.

7. Rutler, "Newman on Assent," 81.

8. Norris, *Newman and His Theological Method*, 29.

9. Bernard Lonergan, *Method in Theology* (London: Darton, Longman & Todd, 1971), 13–14.

10. Bernard Lonergan, *A Second Collection*, ed. W. F. J. Ryan, S.J., and B. J. Tyrrell, S.J. (London: Darton, Longman & Todd, 1974), 38.

11. Lonergan, *A Second Collection*, 263.

12. Lonergan, *A Second Collection*, 273.

13. Lonergan, *A Second Collection*, 263–78.

14. David M. Hammond, "Imagination and Hermeneutical Theology: Newman's Contribution to Theological Method," *The Downside Review* 106 (1988): 17–34, at 23.

15. Newman's reply, 16 March 1870, see Frederick Crowe, *The Lonergan Enterprise* (Cambridge: Cowley, 1980), xxii.

16. Bernard Lonergan, *Insight: A Study of Human Understanding* (New York: Harper and Row, 1978 [1957]), 530–94.

17. Alan Bloom, *The Closing of the American Mind* (New York: Simon and Schuster, 1987).

18. Lonergan, *Insight*, 729.

Epilogue
Newman: A Toast[1]
Sheridan Gilley

One of Newman's most persistent thoughts is that our lives are a narrative, a story with a meaning; and no one has written more profoundly than Newman about the way in which our moral choices shape our characters and mould us under grace, in the image of the saints as God would have them be. But did Newman himself manifest the heroic virtue of a saint? He himself thought not. Saints save souls or give their bodies to be burned. The writer or scholar is generally in a different case. The intellectual life is spent indoors; it is not a fight for God in the world. Most intellectuals are not saints, and most saints are not intellectuals. As W. H. Auden declared:

> To the man in the street, who I'm sorry to say, is a shrewd observer of life,
> The word intellectual means straight away a man who's untrue to his wife.

Newman put it more mildly: saints are not literary men, they do not write Tales or love the classics. Few are the scholars and thinkers heroic enough to be raised to the altars of the Church. There is no dispute about Newman's literary and intellectual eminence: he cannot escape canonization as a philosopher and writer. Saint or sinner, the magician keeps his magic. The light that never was on sea or land, is over all his words and works. But from that point, there is controversy. For some, his cult is too much a cult of personality, the extension beyond the grave of the graciousness which attracted him followers in life. His

Oxford undergraduates, however, said 'Credo in Newmannum'; they loved him because they thought him a spiritual Julius Caesar, not merely for the wonderful charm of manner embodied in the most effortless of flowing English prose. The difficulty is that while the enchantment is there in the writing, it passes from the writing into Newman's story. One of my former Durham colleagues has spoken in print of the literary power of Newman and of his disciple Dean Church to turn the Oxford Movement, a battle fought with no quarter and no charity, into one of the most attractive legends in English church history. Fascination with Newman lends itself to biography or hagiography, verging sometimes on Newmania: but the issue remains whether we find the life of a saint in the story of the man.

That question is bound up with another, of the righteousness of the cause for which he gave his life. Newman is a minority taste among his intellectual fellow-countrymen, and for good reasons. In the recent Newman lecture series in the University of Oxford, the Chancellor, Lord Jenkins, an agnostic of agnostics, looks at Newman as Newman said a dog looked at a hedgehog: he knows not what to do with it. Newman somehow reminded Jenkins of the tortures of the Inquisition, but there is a deeper cause of the noble lord's unsettlement. Newman is the least likely of saints and heroes for contemporary educated Englishmen, who are secular and liberal and indifferent to Christian faith. Newman was the first Christian to sense and state the shivering loneliness of the Christian in a nation that was losing its religion. He knew our condition before his fellow-Christians, who were more impressed by the contemporary evidence of the great Victorian religious revivals. It was on behalf of a dying Christendom that he became the champion of dogma against secular liberalism and against the all-dissolving, all-corroding skepticism of the intellect in religious enquiries, and that he set out to defend the faith as the mingling of Revelation and mystery, a mystery open only in a degree to reason and ultimately beyond it, grounded in conscience rather than in pure intellect, and in an openness to God in the depths of the human personality. It is no wonder that secular liberals feel unsettled by his continuing intellectual eminence, with his clear-minded insistence that the liberal faith also rests on unproven assumptions, and that it is as perfectly reasonable to be certain about religion as the secular liberal is certain about his liberalism. As to recent English culture, Newman is not a prophet in his own country: he is a glorious failure, in his opposition to the dominant values of our age, and in that he stands for the Gospel paradox which modern England and perhaps modern America have forgotten, that God may triumph in our failure, and fail in our success.

It was in this stance that Newman remains a hero, that as long as the present liberal discontent with religion lasts, he will be fashionable only with those who are out of fashion, for so he was in his beginning. It is true that he became the champion of faith and the enemy of liberalism in the last golden days of that great privileged and religious corporation, the University of Oxford, which was then a place as full and fat as any ancient monastery lying helpless as a prey to the spoiler. Newman's Oxford Movement was conceived out of his love and loyalty to the golden city and out of the love and loyalty of his Oxford friends for one another. But Newman came to the faith not as one of the die-hard two bottle orthodox of the old High Church school, but as a despised otherworldly Evangelical Protestant, of the party which was scorned for the depth and sincerity of its religious professions by the mass of easygoing churchgoing Englishmen. Narrowness was the price of depth, and the young Newman has been described by one sympathetic biographer, Maisie Ward, as a monster. For all the mirth and wit of his large and happy household and for all his deep love of his mother and father and sisters, Newman was one of nature's solitaries, delighting in the angel-faces of the gardens of Ham, shy in strange company, overwhelmed with self-reproaches at his own awkwardness or imagined social slights, and happiest with his books and violin and one much-loved friend, first Bowden, then Froude, then Rogers, then Ambrose St. John, a heart to speak to his heart. It is easy to find the young Newman priggish and genteel, over-fastidious in his love of cleanliness and cold bathing, sanctimonious in his hatred of the drunkenness among his fellow undergraduates, and sometimes less than long-suffering with his two impossible brothers: Charles, who lost a job as a teacher for biting a boy, and Francis, who was to write for the Cardinal the unkindest of epitaphs. Newman was not, one feels, an immediately likeable young man. With what contrition does he confess in old age that having none of the normal young man's taste for cheap cigars and riotous company, there was no merit in his abnormal contempt for them.

The young monster also pored over the numbers in the Books of Daniel and Revelation that proved the Papacy to be Antichrist; but it was then that in a famous conversion at the age of fifteen he embarked on his life-long love affair with God. That strange and mysterious encounter gave him his commitment to a religion of religious experience, even while the intellectual dogmas of Calvinism gave him his love of dogma, so that he was his own man and God's man from the first, and even though all the world should despise him, he would like a Christian persevere against all temptations and trials to the gates of the heavenly Jerusalem:

> There's no discouragement
> Shall make his once relent
> His first avowed intent
> To be a pilgrim.

Here he stood, himself and his Creator. Where was there need for community or Church in the solitary communion in which the young Newman began, in this flight of the alone to the alone? As his Oriel mentor Copleston said, never less alone than when alone. And so arises the charge made ten thousand times against him, that he was a subjective individualist for whom reality was always confined to God and to himself. Like the Quaker, he began with the Inner Light, which then became the Kindly Light before his path, to make him irresistible to Catholics who would otherwise be Quakers. Yet it was to just such a solitude that Newman refused to be confined as he grew out of Protestant individualism into the collective communion of the Catholic tradition, as he sought to complement his religion of individual experience and intellectual dogma with an institutional form, a kingdom, a royal priesthood, and a community of hearts and minds in which all hearts and minds might be one.

In this Newman is the great gift of the Protestant tradition to the Catholic Church, the solitary great-heart who recognized the echo of his own voice when he came to read the early Christian Fathers and saw the indomitable Athanasius of Alexandria standing alone against the world. Yet that introduction to the Fathers came at a price. Newman did not have to give his body to be burned to suffer, and it was nothing less than a triumph of grace over nature that this most sensitive of men should survive his own failure in schools to emerge as a brilliant young Fellow of the most brilliant of Oxford Colleges, Oriel, and then surmount his collapse as an examiner and the anguish of the death of his favorite sister, Mary, to sacrifice a life of academic ease in the sectarian wars of later Georgian England.

When Newman came out of his shell in 1828, there was ferment and crisis in the Protestant world, in Britain as in America. These years saw the explosive growth in the Churches of Protestant Nonconformity, and gave birth to the Plymouth Brethren and the Catholic Apostolic Church, to Mormons and Adventists and Transcendentalists. They also witnessed the crisis of the Church of England, the admission of Roman Catholics to the British Parliament and the beginning of the death of the British Confessional State, the State offering a privileged monopoly of citizenship to the members of the Established Church. In a nation in religious ferment but still sure it was Protestant, in which the Church of England knew that she was Protestant almost before she knew that she was Christian, in which Protestants hated Popery not knowing if it were a man or a horse, Newman found in the early Christian Fathers the inspiration to recatholicize the Church of England, to restore her authority as the Catholic Church of Christ and to recover the principle of life and growth to renew her strength and triumph over her enemies.

There was in Newman that mixture of fierceness and sport

which made him too partisan, too immature. But the very immaturity was transcended in the self-doubtings attendant on his illness in the lovely serene land of Sicily, which he later recorded in one of the strangest documents even penned, a mental pilgrimage in delirium through a landscape of nightmare. He had, he decided, not sinned against light after all; and while becalmed in an orange boat in the Straits of Bonifacio, he wrote of his Kindly Light, and returned to battle for the faith of England and Oxford. All Newman needed for his fight were a pulpit, and books and friends; all were given, and in a wonderful outpouring of literature, in a mere eight years, the classic years of the Tractarian or Oxford Movement, between 1833 and 1841, Newman quite simply rethought the theology and devotional life of the Church of England.

Here was the heroism of the scholar. *The Arians of the Fourth Century* and *The Church of the Fathers* made patristics live with the vividness of the contemporary novel. The *Tracts for the Times* recalled the Church to a militant Catholic understanding of Church and ministry and sacrament, the poetry of the *Lyra Apostolica* taught the English nation a new devotional music. The *Parochial Sermons* conveyed the utter reality of God, as from one who knew Him in the uttermost recesses of the heart and will, and explored them with the finesse of touch of a surgeon of the spirit, sometimes with a severity that hurt in the brooding sense of the power of sin and the need for the Law's stern fires to combat it. The *University Sermons* defined conscience and not reason as the source of our knowledge of God in the sense of obligation to Him as our lawgiver and judge, and gave a new precision and breadth to the understanding of the relations between faith and reason. The *Lectures on the Prophetical Office* redefined the Church of England's Via Media between Rome and popular Protestantism, the *Lectures on Justification* surveyed and transcended those differences between the warring armies of the Reformation and Counter-Reformation which had once divided Europe, "The Tamworth Reading Room" tore to pieces the pretensions of a liberal utilitarian substitution of calculation and knowledge for morality. Then there are the wonderful letters: sometimes silly, as in the occasional misogyny, more often wise and witty, but all with the same authentic voice which is music to the ear and solace to the soul.

And so there is hidden treasure here: the choicest of metaphors, the sharpest of ironies, passages to move to laughter or to tears. What demon moved Newman to wish the comfortable Bishops of the Establishment no better termination of their course than the spoiling of their goods and martyrdom? This passage of Tract 1 was heavily censored in the copy for student use in the newly High Church Durham University, itself founded in 1832 to protect the Church's wealth from radical despoilers, and the pungent language of Tract 1 anticipates the disaster of the last Tract, Tract 90 in 1841, when Newman's attempt to prove that the Anglican 39 Articles could be interpreted in a Catholic sense brought the whole Oxford Movement down upon his head in a great national wave of No Popery. The last Anglican years saw him still steadily at work, with his editions of Fleury and Athanasius, but the climax came with the argument of crowning originality in the *Essay on the Development of Christian Doctrine* that Christian doctrine must develop and grow if it claims to live. It was in this book that Newman attained the height of his spiritual and intellectual vision, for the argument of the *Essay on Development* is nothing less than the projection of his own creative powers of life and growth to nineteen centuries of Christianity. It seems to me the strongest argument for Newman's conversion to Roman Catholicism that he achieved his personal and intellectual maturity in the very act of becoming a Roman Catholic.

Nothing so became his membership of the Church of England as the leaving of it. The hardest part of that departure was the "Parting of Friends," but almost as terrible was the species of social death which then awaited a convert to Rome, in Newman's case, even the loss of surviving family, in the complete severing of contact with one much-loved sister and the partial loss of another. Catholics tried to be kind, though their leader, Nicholas Wiseman, that wonderfully flamboyant purple figure, born to be a Cardinal, undid some of his own undoubted goodwill by insensitivity and inefficiency, not least in bringing Newman near to gaol for libelling a philandering anti-Catholic lecturer and ex-Dominican friar. Newman's own theology, with its distrust of unaided reason and view of a Revelation given at least in part in non-propositional form, seemed fuzzy beneath the blue skies of Italian theology, in which Revelation was a matter of sharp statement of truths as clear as the Roman air.

Newman's former fellow-Anglicans were hurt by the delicious satire of his *Difficulties of Anglican* and *Lectures on the Present Position of Catholics.* The Oratory that Newman established at Birmingham was less fashionable than its daughter house founded in London by Newman's disciple Frederick Faber. As with Paul and Barnabas, an enmity rose between them: so also an enmity arose between Newman and the coming light of the Catholic Church in England, Wiseman's favorite Anglican convert Henry Edward Manning. Newman's period as first Rector of the Catholic University of Ireland was brought to an end in part by the quarrels of the Irish, a projected translation of the Bible came to nothing, and when he tried to assist the Liberal Catholic John Acton's periodical *The Rambler*, his essay on the Church's need to consult the lay faithful was episcopally delated to Rome. It is true that these years had their triumphs in the works which became *The Idea of a University*, the attempt to define a Christian humanism which was in a good sense liberal, and to separate and synthesize the ideals of the Christian and the gentleman, Hellas and Judaea, Athens and Jerusalem. Yet Newman's experience of Catholicism was increasingly one of happiness in his faith and unhappiness in everything else. Even his Oratory, with few new members, seemed a failure. Here, it seemed, was the justification of the Protestant charge of the genius wasted on Rome. Was there nothing left for him but death?

The whole world knew the story of the astonishing resurrection from an obscurity worse than the grave of that sad, defeated, exhausted old man, who when Charles Kingsley, himself a man of genius, attacked his honesty, replied in the *Apologia* with so ferociously sincere a retelling of his own life that as with Horatius of old, some of the very enemy applauded:

> And when above the surges
>   They saw his crest appear,
> All Rome sent forth a rapturous cry,
> And even the ranks of Tuscany
>   Could scarce forbear to cheer.

The *Apologia* is, however, a great work for a still greater reason, that it showed Newman coming to terms with the Protestant and liberal elements in himself: a species of self-reconciliation that closely followed on the mending of old Anglican friendships, and made John Henry Newman a man of whom his fellow-countrymen of all parties and churches could feel proud.

Even this popularity was costing, however, for it also made Newman the figurehead and symbol of those Catholics who disliked the personality cult of Pope Pius IX and the increasing Italianization, Romanization and Ultramontanization of the Roman Catholic Church in England and the centralization of all authority over the wider Church in Rome. Having been a reactionary Catholic to Protestants, Newman seemed a dangerous liberal to some Catholics. A reactionary to Anglicans, a liberal to Catholics: Newman became a symbolic arch-rival to Manning who torpedoed Newman's plan to set up an Oratory at Oxford, and took an unkind pleasure in joking about his butler, also called Newman, and was in the habit in his old age of numbering Dr. Newman's heresies on his long tapering fingers. While personally believing in papal infallibility, Newman achieved an unwitting prominence in his opposition to the opportuneness of having it defined, and Manning may have tried to prevent Rome from giving Newman a Cardinal's hat by a none too clever piece of trickery. These old battles between men who were generally good men lend an epic air to Victorian Catholic history, and the personalities involved, somehow larger than life, still live on in the ecclesiastical imagination, fired at the last by the grant to Newman of the cardinal's hat: again Newman went to Italy to receive it and again as in his youth, nearly died there.

There is certainly an ironic splendor to Newman's final triumph in a blaze of sacred purple glory; perhaps even more splendid was almost the last great intellectual triumph, *An Essay in Aid of a Grammar of Assent*, with its attempt to show that religious certitude is no more than democratic common sense, built upon the discovery of what is concrete and real, so that the ordinary believer has as much right as Lord Jenkins to his certitudes, perhaps an even better one. One last great work, the Preface to *The Via Media*, rethought Catholic ecclesiology, and defined the balance and tension among the Prophetical, Priestly and Regal Offices in the Church, as among the devotional, intellectual and institutional aspects of the religious life itself.

The natural instinct of the man of conservative imagination is to feel in the presence of such a life not worthy to untie Newman's shoes. Yet Newman was quite content, so he said, to be a boot black to the saints; and I think that his wonderful irony would come into play were we to treat him with overreverence. It is that irony that can preserve us from overdogmatism, even one from Durham: the insistence of the author of the *Prophetical Office* that the marrow of Christian believing lies in the Catholic creeds; the minimalist who made a wise and gentle minimal view of papal infallibility comprehensible if not acceptable to his Protestant fellow-countrymen; who defended Transubstantiation by declaring that he knew as much and as little about substance as the wisest philosopher, and who insisted that while Christ died as an Atonement for human sin, we have only human reasons why he did so. He loved a certain playfulness about his own favorite saint, Philippo Neri. At one crisis of his youthful fortunes, he remembered chiefly that he found his tutor eating fried parsley. Even his defense of the intellectual or theological element in the Church, as of the intellect itself, is touched by a sense of its limitations. He would be the first to confess that great saints are not impeccable, and great theologians are not infallible. Newman did change and grow, even if there were faults which he did not wholly overcome. Let us not lose sight of the humanity of the scholar so fastidious as to be knocked off his chair by a schoolboy's false pronunciation in Greek, who was equally anxious that the young gentlemen in his charge should eat their mutton scraps but who was not too proud to play the fiddle with his schoolboys. The danger of hagiography is of treating Newman as if his life and thought were perfect wholes permitting no dissent and no criticism; the splendor of a true hagiography should be to see him in his flesh and blood humanity. Let us heed his own passion for reality, amid the sooty brickwork and industrial squalor of Victorian England, with its limes and laurels and carriage folk and sweaty suffering poor. There is more to Newman than the avatar of timeless Catholic truth. On a thousand things, he is the point of departure for discussion, not its terminus, the endlessly inspiring and infinitely suggestible teacher linking the ancient and modern worlds of thought. He has left us a body of still living ideas: the development of doctrine, the illative sense, and right of theologians and the laity to a place in the ecclesiastical sun, the personal character of religious truth, the primacy of experience over pure intelligence, the limits of reason and the limits of authority. His greatness, however, is no more nor less than that of any other Christian who has to overcome sorrow and suffering to do the work that God wants him to do. Indeed Newman has to be judged in this by a higher standard than most, only because he was raised up to do so great a work as a Prophet to unheeding Israel; we judge him glorious for his achievement, not for his perfection. Newman was a saint, in the most primary and primitive of senses, that as a simple Evangelical Christian, under the difficulties of a temperament both sensitive and severe, he did the work that God wanted him to do. His very writings were the answer to an external call; their beauty of form was the product of the struggle to say what he wished to say for God, as clearly as possible. They soar for a purpose, to lift us to our Maker. The *Grammar of Assent* was the first of Newman's works not called forth by special need or circumstance; and even that work, the summary of a lifetime's thought, was written not for self but for the Almighty lover:

I do not ask to see
The distant scene, one step enough for me.

For all of us who need lights to light our path, John Henry
Newman is a bearer of light, to show us where our Kindly Light
is leading. May we at the last follow him from shadows and
images into truth. In that spirit, I give you the toast, John Henry
Newman.

Notes

1. This essay was presented as the Banquet Address at Saint
Louis University's Newman Centenary Conference, fall 1990.

Appendix
A Connected View of Old and New

An Address by Lawrence H. Biondi, S.J.
President of Saint Louis University[1]

"The Intellectual Ethos of John Henry Newman" is the challenging title of this conference, celebrated by many scholars of international repute from Britain and continental Europe as well as from Canada and the United States. As the President of Saint Louis University, I am honored to contribute this address to the celebration of Newman's thought in the centenary year of his death.

The title of my address is, "a connected view of old and new," a phrase from Newman's sixth university discourse from 1852 when he was planning the opening of the new Catholic university in Dublin. Newman became the first rector of that university and his university discourses became the first part of his book, *The Idea of a University*, that remains so well known in academic circles today. In 1841, almost a decade prior to his Dublin university discourses, he made a similar remark in his fourteenth *University Sermon* on "Wisdom": he explained that "wisdom in conduct or policy implies a connected view of the old and the new."[2]

This connection between old and new provides a fascinating insight into Newman's thought and personality. For example, at the very time he was tutoring students in the Greek and Latin classics, he energetically studied and attended lectures in the brand new science of geology. This gives us a glimpse into one of his lifelong concerns: that the search for religious truth required relating the Church of the early Fathers in a meaningful way to nineteenth century experience.

Newman had immense confidence in a university's capability to unite the old and the new. His determination to combine received tradition with novel theories created an openness in his mind that distinguished him from many of his peers. For example, this openness was evident in his fascination with Darwin's theory of the evolution of species, a theory that threatened and appalled so many other religious-minded thinkers of his day.

We celebrate this intellectual openness and vigor of Newman's thought in many interdisciplinary papers. The interesting variety of these themes encapsulates and represents the interdisciplinary enterprise of research, writing and teaching that the Jesuit ethos of our university upholds.

This Newman centenary celebration coincides with other anniversary celebrations at our university: the 500th anniversary of the birth of Saint Ignatius of Loyola, the founder of the Society of Jesus, and the 450th anniversary of that founding. These Jesuit anniversaries honor the vigor and plurality of thought that characterized Newman's exciting life.

The topics of the conference papers suggest how much Newman was a counter-cultural figure in his own society. Today we are inspired by his remarkable skill for developing the old while embracing the new. "Growth is the only evidence of life" he told us. Our scholarly task, then, is to nurture that growth in our academic endeavors.

The conference theme, "the intellectual ethos of Newman," is indeed timely. A vibrant, intellectual ethos characterizes not only the greatness of Newman but also expresses the dedication and commitment that each of us struggles to make to academic life. Let us celebrate the thought and personality of this gentle giant from the nineteenth century. And let us hope that our contributions to interdisciplinary scholarship, following his example, truly yield "a connected view of old and new."

Notes

1. This opening address of the Newman Centenary Conference at Saint Louis University was delivered on November 29, 1990. The text was written by Gerard Magill, one of the conference organizers.

2. *Newman's University Sermons. Fifteen Sermons Preached before the University of Oxford, 1826–43*, with introductory essays by D. M. MacKinnon and J. D. Holmes (London: S.P.C.K., 1970), 287.

Bibliography

Works of Newman

The Longmans uniform edition of Newman's works, 1868–81, 36 vols.

Apologia Pro Vita Sua. Edited by David Delaura. New York: W. W. Norton, 1968.

Apologia Pro Vita Sua. Edited, introduction, and notes by Martin J. Svaglic. Oxford: Clarendon Press, 1967.

My Campaign in Ireland, Part I. Catholic University Reports and Other Papers, Printed for Private Circulation Only. Aberdeen: A. King, 1896.

Catholic Sermons of Cardinal Newman. Edited at the Birmingham Oratory. London, 1957.

On Consulting the Faithful in Matters of Doctrine. Edited with an introduction by John Coulson. London: Geoffrey Chapman, 1961.

An Essay in Aid of a Grammar of Assent. Edited, introduction, and notes by I. T. Ker. Oxford: Clarendon Press, 1985.

An Essay in Aid of a Grammar of Assent. Introduction by Étienne Gilson. Garden City, NY: Doubleday & Company, 1955.

An Essay in Aid of A Grammar of Assent. Edited by Nicholas Lash. Notre Dame: University of Notre Dame Press, 1979.

An Essay on the Development of Doctrine. Notre Dame, IN: University of Notre Dame Press, 1989.

Callista: A Tale of the Third Century. London: Burns and Oates, no date.

Discussions and Arguments on Various Subjects. 4th. ed. London: Pickering, 1882.

Historical Sketches. Westminster, Md.: Christian Classics, Inc., 1970.

The Idea of a University. Edited, introduction, and notes by I. T. Ker. Oxford: Clarendon Press, 1976.

The Idea of a University. Introduction by George N. Shuster. Garden City, NY: Doubleday, 1959.

The Idea of a University. Edited by Martin Svaglic. New York: Rinehart and Co., 1960.

John Henry Newman: Autobiographical Writings. Edited by Henry Tristram. New York: Sheed and Ward, 1957.

Lectures on the Present Position of Catholics in England. Addressed to the Brothers of the Oratory, 1851. London: Longmans, Green, 1899.

Letters and Correspondence of John Henry Newman during his Life in the English Church. Edited by Anne Mozley, 2 vols. London: Longmans, Green, 1891.

The Letters and Diaries of John Henry Newman. Edited by C. S. Dessain et al., 31 vols. Vols. I-VI, Oxford: Clarendon Press, 1978-84. Vols. XI-XXII, London: Oxford University Press, 1961-72. Vols. XXIII-XXXI, Oxford: Clarendon Press, 1973-77.

Loss and Gain. London: James Burns, 1848. Reprinted, New York: Garland Press, 1975.

Newman's University Sermons. Fifteen Sermons Preached before the University of Oxford, 1826-43. Introductory essays by D. M. MacKinnon and J. D. Holmes. London: S.P.C.K., 1970.

Parochial and Plain Sermons. 8 vols. London: Longmans, Green, 1891.

The Philosophical Notebook of John Henry Newman, 2 vols. Edited by Edward J. Sillem. Louvain: Nauwelaerts Publishing House, 1969.

The Theological Papers of John Henry Newman on Faith and Certainty. 2 Vols. Edited by Hugo M. de Achaval and J.Derek Holmes. Oxford: Clarendon Press, 1976.

The VIA MEDIA of the Anglican Church. Edited, introduction, and notes by H. D. Weidner. Oxford: Clarendon Press, 1990.

Works on Newman

Biemer, Günter. "Religious Education—A Task between Divergent Plausibilities." In *Newman and Modernism.* Edited by H. Jenkins. *Newman Studien,* vol. XIV. Sigmaringendorf: Regio Verlag Glock & Lutz, 1990.

————. "Stufen des Glaubens. Newmans Treue zur inneren Stimme." In *Gottes Word-Antwort des Menschen.* Edited by G. Greshake. Wurzburg: Echter, 1991.

Blehl, Vincent, F. "Prelude to the Making of a Saint," *America* 160/9 (March 11, 1989): 213–16.

Bouyer, Louis. *Newman: His Life and Spirituality.* New York: P. J. Kenedy and Sons, 1958.

Coulson, John. *Religion and Imagination.* Oxford: Clarendon Press, 1981.

Dessain, Charles Stephen. *John Henry Newman.* Second edition. Stanford, CA: Stanford University Press, 1971.

Evans, G. R. "Newman's Letters to Charles," *The Downside Review* 100 (1982): 92–100.

David M. Hammond, David, M. "Imagination and Hermeneutical Theology: Newman's Contribution to Theological Method," *The Downside Review* 106 (1988): 17–34.

Ker, Ian. *John Henry Newman: A Biography.* Oxford: Clarendon Press, 1988.

Magill, Gerard, ed. *Discourse and Context: An Interdisciplinary Study of John Henry Newman.* Carbondale, IL: Southern Illinois University Press, 1993.

————. "Imaginative Moral Discernment: Newman on the Tension Between Reason and Religion," *The Heythrop Journal* XXXII (1991): 493-510.

————. "Newman's Personal Reasoning: The Inspiration of the Early Church," *Irish Theological Quarterly* 58/4 (1992) 305–13.

————. "Newman on Liberal Education and Moral Pluralism," *Scottish Journal of Theology* 45 (1992): 45–64.

————. "Moral Imagination in Theological Method and Church Tradition: John Henry Newman," *Theological Studies* 53 (1992): 451–75.

————. "Interpreting Moral Doctrine: Newman on Conscience and Law," *Horizons* 20/1 (1993): 7–22.

Norris, Thomas, J. *Newman and His Theological Method: A Guide for the Theologian Today.* Leider, Netherlands: E. J. Drill, 1977.

Rutler, George, W. "Newman on Assent to Religious Belief." In, George W. Rutler, *Christ and Reason: An Introduction to Ideas from Kant to Tyrrell.* Front Royal, VA: Christendom Press, 1990.

Sugg, Joyce. *A Packet of Letters.* London: Oxford University Press, 1983.

Trevor, Meriol. *The Pillar of the Cloud.* London: Macmillan, 1962.

Walgrave, Jan-Hendrik. *Newman the Theologian.* London: Geoffrey Chapman, 1960.

Ward, Wilfred. *The Life of John Henry Cardinal Newman.* 2 vols. London: Longmans, Green, 1913.

Zeno, Fr. O.F.M. *Newman's Inner Life.* San Francisco: Ignatius Press (1952), 1987.

Other Works

Arnold, Matthew. *Culture and Anarchy, with Friendship's Garland and Some Literary Essays.* Ed. R. H. Super, in *The Complete Prose Works of Matthew Arnold.* Ann Arbor, MI: University of Michigan Press, 1965.

————. *Dissent and Dogma.* Ed. R. H. Super. Ann Arbor, MI: The University of Michigan Press, 1968.

————. *Lectures and Essays in Criticism*. Ed. R. H. Super. Ann Arbor, MI: The University of Michigan Press, 1973.

————. *Mixed Essays*. Ed. R. H. Super. Ann Arbor, MI: The University of Michigan Press, 1972.

Bennett, J. G. *Enneagram Studies*. York Beach, Me: Samuel Weiser Press, 1983.

Bennett, Tony. *Formalism and Marxism*. New York: Methuen, 1979.

Berger, P. L. *The Heretical Imperative: Contemporary Possibilities of Religious Affirmation*. Garden City, NY: Doubleday, 1979. *Zwang zur Haresie*, German ed. Frankfurt: S. Fischer, 1980.

Berger, P. L., T. Luckmann. *The Social Construction of Reality. A Treatise in the Sociology of Knowledge*. New York: Doubleday, 1966.

Bloom, Alan. *The Closing of the American Mind*. New York: Simon and Schuster, 1987.

Carlyle, Thomas. *Sartor Resartus: The Life and Opinions of Herr Teufelsdröckh*. Ed. Charles Frederick Harrold. New York: Odyssey, 1937.

Crowe, Frederick. *The Lonergan Enterprise*. Cambridge: Cowley, 1980.

Egan, Kieran. *Educational Development*. New York: Oxford University Press, 1979.

Erikson, E. H. *Identitat und Lebenszyklus*. Frankfurt: Suhrkamp, 1966.

Fowler, J. *Faith Development and Pastoral Care*. Philadelphia, PA: Fortress Press, 1987.

Fowler, J., S. Kean. *Life-maps. Conversations on the Journey of Faith*. Texas: Word Books, 1978.

Fowler, J., K. E. Nipkow, F. Schweitzer. *Glaubensentwicklung und Erziehung*. Gütersloh: Güterslohcr Verlagshaus Gerd Mohn, 1989.

Froude, James Anthony. *Short Studies of Great Subjects*, Fourth Series. New York: C. Scribner's Sons, 1905.

Heilbrun, Carolyn. *Toward a Recognition of Androgyny*. New York: Harper and Row, 1973.

Kellner, Hans. *Language and Historical Representation: Getting the Story Crooked.* Madison, WI: University of Wisconsin Press, 1989.

Lonergan, Bernard. *Insight: A Study of Human Understanding.* New York: Harper and Row (1957), 1978.

————. *Method in Theology.* London: Darton, Longman & Todd, 1971.

————. *A Second Collection.* Ed. W. F. J. Ryan, S.J., and B. J. Tyrrell, S.J. London: Darton, Longman & Todd, 1974.

Mill, John Stuart. *Autobiography and Literary Essays.* Toronto: University of Toronto Press, 1981.

Miller, J. Hillis. *Fiction and Repetition: Seven English Novels.* Cambridge: Harvard University Press, 1982.

Newman, Jay. "The Motivation of Martyrs: A Philosophical Perspective," *The Thomist* 35 (1971): 581-600.

Nipkow, K. E., Schweitzer, F., Fowler, J. *Glaubensentwicklung und Erziehung.* Gütersloh: Gütersloher Verlagshaus Gerd Mohn, 1989.

Oser, F. *Wieviel Religion braucht der Mensch? Erziehung und Entwicklung zur religiosen Autonomie.* Gütersloh: Gütersloher Verlagshaus Gerd Mohn, 1988.

Oser, F., P. Gmunder. *Der Mensch-Stufen seiner religiosen Entwicklung. Ein strukturgenetischer Ansatz.* Zurich: Benzinger, 1984.

Riso, Don Richard. *Personality Types: Using the Enneagram for Self-Discovery.* Boston, MA: Houghton Mifflin Company, 1987.

Trollope, Anthony. *He Knew He Was Right.* London: World's Classics edition, Oxford University Press, 1985.

Notes on Contributors

Günter Biemer is a professor of Religious Education in the Faculty of Theology at the University of Freiburg. He specializes in Newman studies, Christian-Jewish dialogue, Catechetics of the Sacraments, and Didactics. His publications include: *Newman on Tradition* (1967); *Internat. Cardinal Newman Studien*, co-editor with H. Fries and W. Becker (1980-); *Katechetik der Sakramente* (1983, 1987); *John Henry Newman (1801-1890). Leben und Werk* (1989).

Marie Brinkman, S.C.L., is a professor of English and Chair of the Department of Language and Literature at Saint Mary's College, Leavenworth, Kansas. She graduated from the University of Wisconsin, and she specializes in Newman studies, 19th century British literature, and literary theory and criticism. Her publications include: "Toward a Theology of Religious Life," *Review for Religious* (1971); "On Teaching and Learning," *Columbia Teachers College Bulletin* (1978); "Liberal Learning for the Working Adult," *North Central Association Quarterly* (1987).

Ronald R. Burke is a professor in the Department of Philosophy and Religion, the University of Nebraska at Omaha. He graduated from Yale University, and he specializes in modern Catholic thought. His publications include: "An Orthodox Modernist with a Modern View of Truth," *Journal of Religion* (1977); "Loisy's Faith: Landshift in Catholic Thought," *Journal of Religion* (1980); "Was Loisy Newman's Modern Disciple?" in *Newman and the Modernists*, ed. Mary Jo Weaver (1985); *John Henry Newman: Theology and Reform* (1992), ed.

Edward Enright, O.S.A., is a visiting assistant professor in the Department of Theology at Villanova University. He graduated from The Catholic University of America, and he specializes in Newman studies and in historical theology (19th and 20th centuries).

Sheridan Gilley is a Reader in Theology in the Department of Theology at the University of Durham, England. He graduated from Cambridge University, and he specializes in modern Church history. His publications include: *The Irish in the Victorian City*, co-editor, (1985); *The Irish in Britain 1815-1939* (1989); *Newman and His Age* (1990).

Eugene Hollahan is a professor in the Department of English at Georgia State University, Atlanta. He graduated from the University of North Carolina, and he specializes in literary criticism, Victorian literature, the study of Gerard Manley Hopkins, and the Novel. He is editor of the journal, *Studies in the Literary Imagination*, and his publications include: *Crisis-Consciousness and the Novel* (1992); *Hopkins Against History* (1994).

Ian Ker is the Dean of graduate research at Maryvale Institute, Birmingham, England. He graduated from Cambridge University, and he specializes in Newman studies. His publications include: *John Henry Newman: A Biography* (1988); *The Achievement of John Henry Newman* (1990); *Newman and the Fullness of Christianity* (1993); *Healing the Wound of Humanity: The Spirituality of John Henry Newman* (1993).

Harvey Kerpneck is a professor and the Discipline Representative (Chair) in the Department of English at St. Michael's College, the University of Toronto. He graduated from the University of Toronto, and he specializes in literary theory, and Victorian prose, poetry and fiction. His publications include: *Undergraduate Education in English in Canada*, co-author; and many articles on Arnold, Trollope, Meredith, and others.

Gerard Magill is an associate professor in the Department of Theological Studies at Saint Louis University, Saint Louis. He graduated from Edinburgh University, and he specializes in Newman studies and Moral Theology. His publications on Newman include: *Discourse and Context: An Interdisciplinary Study of John Henry Newman* (1993), ed.

Michael Martin is a visiting assistant professor in the Department of Theology at Boston College. He graduated from the University of Michigan, and he specializes in the history of modern theology, theology and modernity/post-modernity, and Newman studies His publications include: "How was I to be certain? Historical Reasoning as Inferential Investigation in Newman's Conversion," *Theological Studies* (forthcoming).

Jay Newman is a professor in the Department of Philosophy at the University of Guelph, Canada. He graduated from York University, and he specializes in the philosophy of religion and culture. His publications include: *Foundations of Religious Tolerance* (1982); *The Mental Philosophy of John Henry Newman* (1986); *Fanatics and Hypocrites* (1986); *The Journalist in Plato's Cave* (1989); *On Religious Freedom* (1991).

Carla Mae Streeter, O.P., is an associate professor of Systematic Theology at the Aquinas Institute of Theology, St. Louis. She graduated from Regis College and the Toronto School of Theology (jointly) and from the University of Toronto. She specializes in Lonergan studies, and systematic theology and spirituality. Her publications include current work on, *A Lonergan Primer: a Wordbook of Lonergan Terminology* (forthcoming).

Joyce Sugg is a writer and former lecturer in Education who graduated from Oxford University and from Birmingham University. She specializes in English literature and Newman studies. Her publications include: *Snapdragon in the Wall*, a biography of J.H. Newman (1964); *A Packet of Letters*, an anthology of J.H. Newman's letters (1983).

Joseph H. Wessling is a professor in the Department of English at Xavier University, Ohio. He graduated from Xavier University, Ohio, and he specializes in the study of Flannery O'Connor and British Romanticism. His publications include: "Narcissism in Toni Morrison's *Sula*," *CLA Journal* 31 (1988); "Teaching the Language of the Humanities," *Humanities Education* 11 (1988).